T0148545

THE GOSPEL OF
HOLLYWOOD

THE GOSPEL OF HOLLYWOOD

Godfrey Esoh

THE GOSPEL OF HOLLYWOOD

Copyright © 2019 Godfrey Esoh.

All rights reserved. No part of this book may be used or reproduced by any means, graphic, electronic, or mechanical, including photocopying, recording, taping or by any information storage retrieval system without the written permission of the author except in the case of brief quotations embodied in critical articles and reviews.

Scripture quotations marked NIV are taken from the Holy Bible, New International Version®. NIV®. Copyright © 1973, 1978, 1984 by International Bible Society. Used by permission of Zondervan. All rights reserved. [Biblica]

Scripture quotations marked KJV are from the Holy Bible, King James Version (Authorized Version). First published in 1611. Quoted from the KJV Classic Reference Bible, Copyright © 1983 by The Zondervan Corporation.

iUniverse books may be ordered through booksellers or by contacting:

iUniverse
1663 Liberty Drive
Bloomington, IN 47403
www.iuniverse.com
1-800-Authors (1-800-288-4677)

Because of the dynamic nature of the Internet, any web addresses or links contained in this book may have changed since publication and may no longer be valid. The views expressed in this work are solely those of the author and do not necessarily reflect the views of the publisher, and the publisher hereby disclaims any responsibility for them.

Any people depicted in stock imagery provided by Getty Images are models, and such images are being used for illustrative purposes only. Certain stock imagery © Getty Images.

ISBN: 978-1-5320-7416-5 (sc)
ISBN: 978-1-5320-7417-2 (e)

Library of Congress Control Number: 2019905103

Print information available on the last page.

iUniverse rev. date: 05/02/2019

CONTENTS

PREFACE

In the mid-to-late 1990s, there were only two people in our neighborhood who owned television sets. Our nearest neighbor was my uncle but his house was a no-go zone for us. In fact, the first time in my life when I was treated like an important person and got my first invitation to sit in his living room for a chat was when I was in high school and had just been elected as National President of the Mbatu Students' Association. Further away from our modest home, my friend's father had a small black-and-white television set. He too was a rich man by our local standards, but he at least allowed us the poor kids to take off our shoes, perch on his veranda, and watch the television through the window.

By 1990, a young, dynamic, and upcoming carpenter by name Sunday Fon, had bought the biggest colored television set I had ever seen in my life. Because he was less rich and more people-oriented, all the youths and kids in the neighborhood migrated to his home for TV watching. 1990 was the year of the famous *Italia 90 World Cup* tournament in which Roger Miller, Thomas Nkono, Tataw Stephen, and their peers led Cameroon to the quarter-finals and demonstrated the glory of African football. Ngia Sunday's living room was vast but never big enough to accommodate all of us. The older people took all the seats, and the kids gratefully squatted on the red cemented floor, too grateful to at least have a glimpse of the TV screen.

Our own home did not have electricity, talk less of a television set. My father had his radio set that was powered by batteries. He alone was allowed to manipulate that radio set, on which he listened to the BBC and VoA early in the morning upon waking and late at night upon returning home. Once in a while, he would play his favorite cassette tapes, *Voice of the Cross*, and *Prince Nico Mbarga*. As a kid, I used to share a room with my mother and my two baby followers (a set of twins) while my dad slept in the adjoining room. So, whatever my father listened to, I inadvertently crashed the party.

Throughout my childhood, adolescence, and right to university, television remained a distinguishing marker of social status. The reverence with which television sets were treated in every home I visited reminded me of my inferiority. By the time I graduated from university, I had developed a relationship with computers and books, but not television. I could spend as much time in the library as I wanted, I could sacrifice my meagre pocket allowance to purchase internet time and spend a few hours each week in the cyber-café. When I discovered the treasure in books, and the wonder of the internet, my thirst for knowledge drowned my deprivation of entertainment.

When I first became a higher education instructor, my friend's mother happily allowed me to take on credit a laptop her son had sent from the USA. Although it was a used DELL laptop, its retail value in Cameroon was my full salary for three months. Because we were friends, I was allowed to pay in tiny monthly installments. With a laptop in my possession, I made good use of my two friends, Louis, and Leonard who were computer technicians and cyber-café attendants. Once in a while, they would allow me to browse the internet for free. Other times they would create an account that I could use to browse and then pay at the end of the month. And then most of the times they would download movies and documentaries which I would save on my laptop and watch at home. I still have an emotional attachment to that laptop, not just because it served me for six years, but because I was finally taken to the police because of it. I took too long to complete the payment, and my benefactor's overzealous daughter thought I was unwilling to pay. She couldn't understand why a man with such a 'good job' would need two years to complete payment for a used laptop. If only she had known the world I came from and lived in.

Because I gained exposure to the media world only after I had fallen in love with books and the unlimited fountain of knowledge found on the internet, I began to find television boring. The same object that had stood as a monument of my inferiority for close to 30 years suddenly appeared so shallow. Because the only movies I watched were those downloaded and saved on my laptop, I had to justify the use of bandwidth and storage space by making sure that the movies were not just time wasters but learning experiences. This is how I gradually filtered out the cowboy stuff and tilted toward inspirational, spiritual, historical, and educative movies and documentaries, many of which I found on YouTube.

Today, it makes no difference if you cover one wall of my living room with a television screen. Today we are enticed to pay for cable TV bundles that come with 99 channels or more. I hardly watch more than 3 of them. Today, Hollywood, Nollywood, Bollywood, and so on are bundled up in a Netflix subscription, but even when I want to reward myself with two hours of movie time, I will typically zap through 30 movie summaries before finding one good one that appeals to me.

The mindset that I bring into entertainment is the same mindset that I bring into every experience in life. It is the quest for meaning that has been grafted into my spirit by my childhood and the unique personal story I have created in the course of navigating the rough paths of life from where I was born to where I am today. Left to the environment in which I was born and the circumstances in which I was raised, the logical conclusion would have been a young Cameroonian man struggling with unemployment, debt, mediocrity, and broken dreams like many Africans of my age. But something drastic happened that changed my story. I vehemently refused to die in the same social rank in which I was born, because in my childhood, my mind was already sharp enough to question why my parents were servants to other people's parents. The material deprivation did not bother me much because I did not really know what I was missing, but even at the age of 5 years, I could already perceive this thing called dignity.

My search for meaning and the secret of success took me into religion and spirituality. There I found one piece of the puzzle. In my rich academic career, I got another piece of the puzzle, because being an inquiring mind, I did not limit myself to the curriculum nor did I study just for the sake of obtaining certificates. Since I was thrust into a leadership role at the age of 17years I have since worked with thousands of young people from all sorts of backgrounds, including occupying top management positions in academic institutions of higher learning. This experience in leadership, education and management has also enriched me with one part of the puzzle.

My brother died 20 years ago when he was just about the age at which I am writing this book. He was a genius who had obtained his Ph.D. at the age of 28 on scholarship in Nigeria and had returned home to contribute in building the young University of Buea. I was devastated not only because he was my brother, but also because he was the one that had plucked me out of a public village school and sent me to attend high school in the most prestigious Catholic high school in Anglophone Cameroon. Because he was my model of success at that tender age, his death triggered a quest to understand the deeper meaning of life. I began doubting the God I had been raised to believe in, and my only hope for survival lay in finding out the truth about life that was beyond doctrine, motivation, and material success.

Fifteen years down the line, I had achieved my own share of career success and propelled myself several levels up the social ladder. Then my mother died, and again, I slipped into darkness. The experiences I encountered while grappling with my mother's death turned out to be the 'dark night of the soul' which is the final trial before one's resurrection. It took a series of visions and miraculous experiences, for me to see clearly how all the pieces of the puzzle finally fitted together around a center that had been there all along.

There is a mystical heritage that is embedded in the traditions that our ancestors passed down to us. Coded within the African soul is the same spiritual substance that is enshrined in the pyramids and temples of Egypt. The same people who settled along the Nile and built the temples and pyramids, invented language, science, and civilization thousands of years before the Greek Empire, are the same race that built trade routes across the Sahara to the Atlantic coast, and subsequently spread across the continent establishing kingdoms and civilizations. The fact that African history and spirituality is not written is not such a bad thing after all. These mysteries were encoded in the myths, legends, folklore, traditional ceremonies, institutions, rituals, art, music, sculpture, architecture, healing, and other mystical practices. Through various forms of initiation, the secret has been preserved for thousands of years, and although they are mostly not aware of it, every African soul is heir to this stupendous treasure. The libraries of Alexandria and Timbuktu display but a tiny fraction of the great treasure that our ancestors have bequeathed to humanity albeit in a covert manner.

So you can see why when I watch a movie, I see that which others are not seeing and hear what others are not hearing. It is the same heightened perception that I bring into every experience, and thereby make it a transformative experience. You may say it is a gift, but I have narrated my story so as to help you understand that it is not some magical power that was bestowed upon me by some unseen force, nor are my deductions merely the fancy of an overactive imagination. The world holds wonders that if your eyes were open to see, you would burst out in tears.

INTRODUCTION

Joy is to the human soul what sunshine is to the earth. Human beings have a natural quest for joy, because it is in a joyful atmosphere that our spiritual, emotional, mental, and physical capacities unfold and blossom at their best. Human society creates entertainment as a means of helping humans relax and be happy, and because of its success in fulfilling this quest, the entertainment industry has become a crucial part of the fabric of human society.

Hollywood has grown to be not only the capital of the global entertainment industry but has somehow been edged on the consciousness of modern man as the monument of vanity. This is why a marriage between the words "Hollywood" and "Gospel" would seem unholy. They appear to be as opposite as night and day. The name Hollywood typically brings to mind the songs, movies, and lifestyles that portray society at its worst – romance, sex, deception, gangs, violence, drugs, fairytales, obscene language, and all the other attributes of fallen humanity. On the other hand, the word "Gospel" brings to mind good news, spiritual wisdom, the message of salvation, and the sacred truths of life. So, the billion-dollar question is, "what good news can come out of Hollywood?".

Among the many social ills that are plaguing modern society, one that stands out most conspicuously is what we may call the entertainment addiction. The millennial generation that are born into the era of satellite television, internet, and social media are the perfect embodiment of this disease. They live and breathe Hollywood. Because Hollywood is the psychological home of billions of people, Hollywood movies, songs, gossips and lifestyles have become the most efficient vehicle for social conditioning. As people become fascinated by these songs, movies, and celebrity lifestyles and immerse themselves into them in the name of innocent entertainment, they unknowingly cast themselves into a hypnotic state in which their subconscious minds become systematically conditioned by the content they persistently expose themselves to.

The guns, drugs, foul language, nudity, flashy houses and cars, gangs, and fairytale romance have tended to jump out of the movies into our lives, our homes, our schools, and our communities. The progressive insanity of our society is in part thanks to Hollywood. But its power to destroy society is its same power to heal and bless society, if this power is put to right use. Indeed, there are a few men and women who have discovered that the grip that Hollywood has on society can be a blessing in disguise.

I have come to realize what a blessing it was to have grown up in a home without a television set. It is only after I had completed university and started working that I could afford my own computer and television. By this time, I had known enough to be selective about what I watched. I have never liked horror and science fiction movies because anything that does not appear natural, like the awful looking extra-terrestrial creatures, gives me nightmares. When I became a parent seven years ago, the need to protect my home from the violent and negative media became more urgent. What started as an innocent desire to resist the temptation of every new movie release and carefully selecting only movies that made me feel inspired and empowered, led to the discovery of a staggering new reality.

There is more to Hollywood than meets the eye. Both deliberately or unconsciously, some movie creators are packaging and transmitting messages of epic value. I was thrilled when I figured out how and why this happens. The creative process involved in conceiving and writing a story makes use of the imagination. Using the process of synthetic imagination, you can research and write a story the way journalists do. The majority of movies are a synthesis of familiar images from the environment, crafted into a new storyline. In fact, most of the time, for every one thousand movies there is only one story retold over and over again in a different setting with a different cast, and with one or two twists. That is why any avid movie fan can predict how a movie will end after watching the first five scenes.

There are a few creators who go beyond the synthetic imagination and make use of the creative imagination. The creative imagination is the natural habitation of the poet, the painter, and the inventor. Those who slip into this domain in the writing process every now and then become channels of some flashes of inspiration. That is why in their movies nuggets of inspiration and spiritual insight will pop up every now and them. They usually do not do it deliberately, so the insights are not consistent.

Then we have the sages who know what I now know. They are mystics and spiritual teachers who have figured out that by infiltrating Hollywood with the spiritual truths that can free the human soul, they could accomplish more than some churches do. Hollywood has a magnetic effect on billions of people, so in terms of numbers it is the biggest church on earth, and in terms of receptivity, it has the most hypnotized audience on earth. Any spiritual truth that is packaged into a Hollywood blockbuster movie without appearing to be spiritual truth, is sure to be received gladly. Thus, we are increasingly seeing the emergence of a new breed of knights or crusaders, whose quest is to enlighten human souls using the medium of entertainment.

This is a secret that Jesus knew and demonstrated. He went to the synagogue and temple only occasionally. Most of his teaching and works were done outdoors among the people. He made friends with fishermen and prostitutes, dined with tax collectors, attended weddings and funerals, and wherever there were people, he went.

As Hollywood now lives with us in our beds, bathrooms, kitchen tables, living rooms, cars, offices, and wherever our televisions and smartphones go, the knights of our time have emerged with the quest to use this Hollywood fever as a means of communicating the secret of the ages. As has been the story of humanity for all time, the treasures we seek are always hidden in plain sight. There is a new trend in which pearls of inspiration and profound spiritual insights are being coded into the songs we listen to and the movies and TV shows we watch – even children's cartoons. The philosophy is that we learn best when we are playing, and these grains of truth reach our subconscious most efficiently when we are unaware of them and are not actively rationalizing and judging.

I had always suspected that this was going on, because after watching some movies, I would feel a surge within me, not the fleeting fun and distraction that movies are intended to bring, but an illuminating and empowering experience. At first, I ignored it, then it started happening too frequently for me to take it for granted, so I decided to pay attention. Then when I watched the movie "National Treasure", a light bulb went off inside of me, and the pattern emerged. I now knew for sure what I had only suspected for years. There are movies from Hollywood which on the surface are fiction and entertainment, but which are loaded with sacred truths waiting for those who are ready to receive them. Although the realization occurred over ten years ago, I decided to keep an eye on Hollywood and watch the progression of this pattern until I was convinced that there were a significant number of movies that one could place in this category of *transcendental entertainment.*

My mother gave birth to 10 of us; 6 girls and 4 boys. I am the last boy (followed by a set of twins). My dad spent the greater part of his active years in Nigeria where he did catering for a number of British colonial administrators, and eventually an American diplomat. In the mid-1970s he succumbed to family pressure and took an early retirement from Nigeria. When he returned to Cameroon, he had no pension, no investments, and no house of his own. While we lived in our family compound dad went to work for his cousin who owned a bakery.

One night, he was trekking home from work dressed in his Kaki overalls and carrying a bunder of used zinc on his head. We had just finished building our house with mud-bricks made by us, and he was collecting used zinc to help seal the many windows that did not yet have covers. That night, on his way from work, he was hit by a speeding vehicle. His solid kaki coat got caught up by a piece of metal underneath the car and he was dragged over a long distance before the coat was detached. His bones were crushed and his body deformed. But he miraculously stayed alive.

I was 8 years old when this accident happened, and dad was 61. It took painfully long for dad to get on his feet again. Taking turns to take care of him at home after he had been discharged from the hospital was my first experience with nursing. Dad finally made it, but he could never do any hard work again. Mom turned us into an army of farm laborers. My father's brother who had brought him back from Nigeria offered her capital to do petty trading in the Bamenda Main Market but she turned down the offer.

According to her, spending all her days in the market was the perfect recipe for keeping us hungry and pushing us into mischief. She trusted the farm more, saying that children who are hungry cannot study. Her mother had raised her on the farm, so although she was the Lagos Lady of the community, she chose to return to the farms on which she had been raised. That is how we became an army of farmers in our tender age. Our struggles as a family, and the work ethic that was grafted into us by our parents, instilled in us the virtues of love, unity, and service to one another. I learned as much from the farm as I learned in school. And as I grew up, what I had considered to be suffering in my childhood turned out to be my best teacher.

Considering the circumstances of my birth, I was quite frankly an unlikely candidate for a decent life, talk less of an epitome of significant success. Yet at the age of thirty-six, I had become a successful medical scientist and educator who travelled out of my country on an annual basis, a husband to an adorable woman, a father to two amazing kids, an influential community leader, and a college (polytechnic) president.

My personal struggles had led me into a spiritual transformation from which I had emerged as a messenger bearing a very unique message – ancient spiritual truths proven by recent scientific evidence, validated by my personal experience, and articulated in modern familiar language. Since this transformation occurred, it has been my life's mission to inspire and empower billions of people all over the world to awaken to the divinity within them, live lives of love, joy, and abundance, and attain the glorious destiny that lies in wait for mankind. Material success is not the goal of life. All things come to those who have found their purpose and are living it.

My new adventure which I have chosen to call *The Gospel of Hollywood* is a project to leverage my gift to decipher these coded spiritual messages and convey them to the public in book form so that the billions of people around the world who are fascinated by these movies, may be carried on the wings of this fascination, to the secret place where the treasures of life are waiting to be found and relished. "National Treasure" deserves to be the first in this series of works that will go on for a very long time.

I am privileged to be able to generate a new idea that can add a new dimension to the traditional conversation of Hollywood. There are those who immerse themselves in movies for the sake of mere entertainment without a care for the views of the academics whose job it is to critique movies based on literary merit. Then there is the big business of Oscars and all the other awards. The *Gospel of Hollywood* perceives movies as vehicles of subliminal communication. The new conversation therefore is about the value of movies to inspire, motivate, and transform people, because after all, this is the ultimate thirst of every human soul.

About the movie - "National Treasure"-

Ever since he was a boy, Gates has been obsessed with finding the legendary Knights Templar Treasure, the greatest fortune known to man. As Gates tries to find and decipher ancient riddles that will lead him to it, he's dogged by a ruthless enemy who wants the riches for himself. Now in a race against time, Gates must steal one of America's most sacred and best guarded documents – the Declaration of Independence – or let it, and a key clue to the mystery, fall into dangerous hands.

Release date
November 19, 2004

Actors
Nicolas Cage: Benjamin Franklin Gates
Sean Bean: Ian Howe
Harvey Keitel: Sadusky
Jon Voight: Patrick Henry Gates
Justin Bartha: Riley Poole
Diane Kruger: Dr. Abigail Chase
Christopher Plummer: John Adams Gates
David Dayan Fisher: Shaw
Oleg Taktarov: Shippen
Erik King: Agent Colfax
Armando Riesco: FBI Agent Hendricks
Stewart Finlay-McLennan Powell
Annie Parisse: Agent Dawes
Stephen A. Pope: Phil
Mark Pellegrino: Agent Johnson
Anne Hathaway: Mia Thermopolis

Writers
Jim Kouf
Marianne Wibberley
Charles Segars
Cormac Wibberley
Oren Aviv

Director
Jon Turteltaub

Official Site
http://movies.disney.com/national-treasure

Note about the transcript excerpts.
The transcript excerpts used in this book was produced directly from watching the movie, with the help of some public domain versions available online (See http://www.script-o-rama.com/movie_scripts/n/national-treasure-script-transcript.html. Accessed 04/20/2019).

CHAPTER 1

The Hidden Treasure

The first insight:

Beyond the material world of eating, drinking, bathing, dressing, walking,
talking, and mating, there is a mental world of waking, sleeping, dreaming.
Beyond the mental world of waking, sleeping, and dreaming, there is a spiritual
world that constitutes the womb of creation, the boundless field in which
unspoken treasures are buried. Those who become masters, heroes, inventors,
and truly successful people are those who tear through the veils of the physical
and mental and dive into the living waters of the spirit.

Ben Gates: *What was his secret?*
John Adams Gates: *A treasure! A treasure beyond all imagining.*

It was an evening in 1974. Young Benjamin Franklin Gates was in the cellar with his grandfather John Adams gates busy. John told Ben a fascinating story about a mysterious treasure. It was the story of the vast treasures that had been accumulated by tyrants, pharaohs, emperors, and warlords. For thousands of years, this treasure had grown to staggering proportions, changing hands every now and then, until at one point, it had simply vanished.

During the first crusade, the knights found a hidden vault in the Temple of Solomon. These knights who found the vaults believed that the treasure was too great for any one man, not even a king. They brought the treasure back to Europe and took the name, "the Knights Templar". Over the next century, they smuggled the treasure out of Europe and formed a new brotherhood known as the "Freemasons", in honor of the builders of the Great Temple.

War followed. By the time of the American Revolution, the treasure had been hidden again. By then, the Masons came to include George Washington, Benjamin Franklin, and Paul Revere. They knew they had to make sure the treasure would never fall into the hands of the British, so they devised a series of clues and maps to its location. Over time the clues were lost or forgotten, until only one remained.

One night in 1832 Charles Carroll, a member of the Masons, was the last surviving signer of the Declaration of Independence. He knew he was dying. He woke up his stable boy in the middle of the night and ordered him to take him to the White House to see Andrew Jackson because it was very urgent that he speak to the President.

He never got the chance to speak with the President because the President wasn't there that night. So, Charles Carroll took into his confidence the one person he could: his stable boy. That stable boy was Thomas Gates, the grandfather of John's grandfather. The young Thomas Gates became the custodian of the last remaining secret to the hidden treasure.

The secret was the phrase "The secret lies with Charlotte". But no one knew who/what Charlotte was. The Masons had devised a system of coding their messages and leaving clues that only the most gifted minds could unravel. This was their way of making sure that the treasure would never fall into the wrong hands. According to John, symbols like the unfinished pyramid, and the all-seeing eye on the dollar bill are all symbols through which the Knights Templar, guardians of the treasure, are all speaking to us.

Ben was fascinated by this tale from his grandfather. His father, Patrick Gates, on the other hand, was skeptical, even annoyed. He said has ancestors had been a family of fools for having believed this tale and spent all their fortune searching for the clues to the treasure. Will Ben share the skepticism of his father and put an end to this madness, or will he allow himself to be contaminated to his grandfather's quest and risk wasting his life away in search for a secret treasure that does not exist?

There is more to life than the circumstances in which we are born. There is more to life than what we are taught in school or what we see on television. There is more to life than chasing the American Dream. Every human soul knows instinctively that the world which we perceive with our five senses is but a shadow of a more glorious reality. This is why desire is the very force of life. From the single celled micro-organism to the galaxies, every life form is animated by the yearning for something more.

Human traditions from ancient times to present are replete with stories about a certain hidden treasure. Whether it is the lost Ark of the Covenant, King Solomon's Mines, or the Holy Grail, it does not matter by what name we call it. Since we all agree that there is more to life than meets the eye and we all are naturally inclined to seek for and possess the secret power with which we can access the higher realms of existence, ranging from personal achievement in the now, to eternal bliss in the afterlife.

The central message of Jesus' teaching is about a hidden treasure, and the whole of Christian life is about finding that hidden treasure; *"The kingdom of heaven is like treasure hidden in a field. When a man found it, he hid it again, and then in his joy went and sold all he had and bought that field." (Matthew 13:44 NIV).* This is same with every other religion on earth. The only difference is the name by which this treasure is called.

The movie National Treasure articulates the premise that the earth is a field in which a treasure is hidden. All humans are treasure hunters, and the glory of life belongs to those who find the treasure. On this premise, all religions and cultures of the earth agree. But the question arises; How many people are consciously aware that there is more to life than what they are currently experiencing? The tragic answer is that 95% of the human race is not consciously searching for the treasure of life. That is why only 5% of humans wind up successful and more than 80% of the wealth of the world winds up in the hands of 1% of the people.

Most humans are barely existing rather than living, because they are not spiritually awake. The average human being does not have a mind of his/her own. They are merely robots set on default mode to express the conditioned responses programmed into them by the collective consciousness of the environment they are exposed to. Mental and spiritual inertia seems to be the gravest sin that has ever befallen humanity.

The plumber's child tends to become a plumber. The kid born in the village tends to live his life in the village. The children of Catholic parents usually remain Catholic all their lives. The children of Democrats are more likely to vote Democrats. Wealth moves along family lines just as poverty moves along family lines. A certain number of universities become noted for producing inventors and Nobel Prize winners and the tradition goes on for centuries. A certain generation invents a social pill called "The American dream" and although their grandchildren are born into a completely different world, the concept of a successful and comfortable life is still "The American dream". Humans in their natural state are slaves to inertia. That is why we need to inundate the mental atmosphere with billions of movies, songs, books, anything that can serve as a trigger to help human beings snap out of the hypnotic state in which they have been sleep-walking through life.

National Treasure is one of those movies that are coded with numerous spiritual insights that have transformative value. My purpose as an author is to bring people into the experience of personal transformation, by inspiring them with spiritual and metaphysical truths. There is a huge difference between self-improvement and transformative living. There is a huge difference between achieving success and experiencing personal transformation.

Transformative Living is an approach to life that focuses on accompanying people through the process of self-inquiry toward having a direct experience of the Truth that they really are. When people have a direct experience of Truth, this Truth becomes a living fountain from which their health, relationships, careers, finances, communities, and societies are spontaneously transformed into the highest version of themselves imaginable.

Transformative Living can best be explained using the metaphor of the Transfiguration in the Bible. In this narrative which we find in the Gospels (Mathew 17:1-8, Mark 9:2-), and Luke 9:28-36), Jesus goes up to the mountain to pray, accompanied by three of his apostles (Peter, James, and John), and is transfigured before them. His face shines like the sun and his clothes become as white as the light. Then Moses and Elijah appear before them and have a conversation with Jesus. Peter says to Jesus, "Lord, it is good for us to be here. If you wish, I will put up three shelters - one for You, one for Moses, and one for Elijah." While he is still speaking, a bright cloud envelopes them, and a voice from the cloud says, "This is My Son, whom I love; with Him I am well pleased. Listen to Him!"

Transformation is what happens when we discover our true identity as Individualizations of the Infinite Being who is Absolute, and Eternal, and beside whom there is no other. This discovery can only take place through an awakening from within. No one can give it to us. The purpose of all religion, all philosophy, and all science is to accompany us on the journey of self-inquiry; that thing called prayer or spirituality. The mountain is a symbol of inner silence. Moses is a symbol of the Law while Elijah is a symbol of the Prophets. No matter our current station in life and no matter what kind of temple we want to build for ourselves, there are always two pillars that lead into that temple; the first pillar is Moses, the law, orthodoxy, tradition, legality, reality as it is. The second pillar is Elijah, prophecy, vision, creativity, innovation, disruption. Jesus' three closest friends represent your three states of consciousness that must blend to form the transformative experience; James stands for the rational mind (reason), Peter stands for the intuitive mind (faith), and John stands for the psycho-motor mind (charity). Transformation happens when that which is known intellectually, is believed in the heart, and then acted upon.

The world of men and women will not see your face literally shining like the sun and your clothes shining like light as was the case with Jesus. Your own light will shine forth through the various areas of your daily life. Faith is when you transcend all dogmatic thought systems (be they scientific, cultural, social, or religious), free yourself from the security of the known, and lose yourself in the unknown, like a drop of water slipping into the sea. When through Faith you become one with Truth, your mind and soul become enlightened and flooded by this Truth. Truth is translated by the mind into wisdom and creativity. Truth is translated by the heart (soul) into love and compassion.

Faith, Reason, and Love, symbolized in the Bible as Peter, James, and John, are the inner qualities of the transformed person. When you have become the Truth on that mountain of Awakened Consciousness, your being becomes the fountain of wisdom and love that flows back downhill to the world, to transform your daily experiences. Life becomes a romantic dance, a spontaneous unfolding of miracles. It becomes as if the universe has become your lover and is living each moment to surprise you with one gift after another that always supersedes what you could ever ask or imagine, and always comes in ways you never could think of.

The hidden treasure of life is really the fullness of who you are as a human being. You are more than the body you carry. You are more than the mind with which you think. You are more than the soul with which you feel. You are more than the beliefs that govern your habitual thoughts, words, feelings, and actions. You are more than the environment you live in, the social conditioning you are subjected to, and the roles you play. The problem of life is that through social conditioning we have forgotten who we truly are, and are busy solving problems, trying to earn a living, and doing everything else that distracts us from the one thing that matters – the treasure that lies within ourselves.

From my earliest days as a Biology student, one of the things that stood out most clearly in my mind was the idea that from the modest single-celled amoeba to the complex human body, every life form is the outer expression of a specific pattern programmed into a genetic code. Similarly, in practical life, there is a recipe for every dish we eat, a blueprint for every house that is built, and a model for every technological gadget that is produced. One of the greatest failures of mankind has been our failure to respect this same universal law and create a pattern of success that we as humans should follow. Little wonder therefore, that less than 5% of humans ever live up to their potential to the degree that they are considered really successful. We have left this most important aspect of our lives to chance, everyone groping in the dark in pursuit of his/her own vague idea of what they consider to be success.

Grounded in the African, Christian, and Scientific traditions I have inherited, my personal experience, and a careful observation of the truly great people in the world has led me to the conclusion that true success is the embodiment of twelve cardinal attributes. Those who have found the hidden treasure spontaneously manifest these qualities:

1. Spiritual Awareness

Truly successful people are spiritually awake. Their sense of identity is rooted in the awareness that they are the individuation of the Infinite Spirit of Life, Love and Power. Therefore, they are one with God, one with the universe, and one with every other human being. From this elevation, they know that life is not about the ego, but rather about how you touch the lives of those around you.

2. Mental Acuity

Truly successful people are mentally alert. By cultivating the habit of study and meditation (reflection) they unfold their mental capacities to optimal levels of intelligence. They are not limited to the myopic worldview grafted into their consciousness by their ancestry, childhood programming, and social conditioning. They are not cloistered into the curriculum that their minds were molded into through formal education.

Truly successful people have developed practical wisdom, through self-directed, lifelong, reflective learning.

3. Emotional Poise

Truly successful people blossom emotionally. They are full of self-confidence and enthusiasm. Their love for life overflows as happiness, joy, peace, laughter, gratitude, optimism, courage, and hope. They bring their positive energy into every environment they enter, and usually have a magnetic effect on people. They do not try to achieve success by artificially cultivating positive mental attitudes. The positive mental attitudes are the spontaneous expression of their real self. They cannot help but glow.

4. Physical Health and Wellbeing

The spiritual source that lights the fire of the soul, provides the light of the mind, and radiates the warmth of the heart, emerges on the outside as a healthy body. Beauty, fitness, and charm are not the result of diets, fitness programs, cosmetics, and designer clothes, but the natural blossoming of the life that is within. The external diets, fitness programs, cosmetics, and designer clothes are not the cause of health and fitness; they are only complementary. Millions of people spend huge sums of money on these programs on a yearly basis and have no results, while there are others who are fit, beautiful, and charming, without reliance on other external system. When you are healthy within, you will be healthy without, even without the help of beauty and fitness programs. When you are sick within, there is no health and fitness program that will be able to help you.

5. Empowering Relationships

Truly successful people are surrounded by happy people. Their circle begins with their love relationships with their significant other, expands to their family, then to their friends, then to their social network, and then the community. They enjoy meaningful relationships with people who love them for who they are, support them without judging, and celebrate them in both happy and dark times.

6. Harmony with Nature

Truly successful people realize that they are one with nature. They support nature and nature supports them. They have a heightened sensitivity to their environment which usually reflects in their affinity for plants, animals, natural environments, and natural lifestyles. They know that the Divine Life that is breathing forth as the splendor of the universe is the same Divine Life that is breathing forth as them.

7. Career Excellence

Truly successful people have a career they thrive in. They do not work for a living, but rather have a career through which they express their specialized knowledge, skills, and passion in a way that serves and enriches as many people as possible. This can be in a conventional profession or entrepreneurship, or a combination of both. The defining quality here is that they find a way of serving as many people as possible by leveraging their super powers.

8. Financial and Material Abundance

Truly successful people experience financial and material abundance as a natural consequence of who they are and what they do. They are not slaves to the paychecks, mortgages, taxes, loans, debts, and credit cards. Money flows to them through multiple channels in ever increasing quantities on a continuous basis.

9. Creative Self-Expression

Truly successful people are spontaneous solution - makers. They do not limit themselves to the current standards and beliefs that govern their line of work or business. Instead, they have the capacity for disruptive thinking through which they frequently generate innovative ideas to make life easier, healthier, richer, and happier for other people. They are a beneficial presence on the planet. The world today and future generations will be better off because they walked this earth.

10. Influence

Truly successful people are always a positive influence in the world because they are changemakers wherever they find themselves. By letting their light shine, they inspire others to allow their light to shine. They recognize that it is not great acts that change the world but little acts that are done with great love. So, they focus on greatness, not fame. They make it a duty to touch one life at a time, one day at a time.

11. Quality Time

Truly successful people have all the time in the world to enjoy all the life they are capable of enjoying. Vacation is not a luxury or obligation but a way of life. Their work hours are not determined by someone else but by them, based on their other priorities. They spend quality time with their loved ones; they have time for study and spiritual growth; they have enough time to give and enrich the lives of others. They do what they want; they have what they want; they go where they want and when they want. They do not worry about the past; they do not fear the future; they make every moment a paradise.

12. Perpetual Growth

Truly successful people experience life as a perpetually increasing, expanding, unfolding, and overflowing adventure. They are always working to build a better version of themselves. They live in the flow of increasing life, and they are a channel of increase for all. Every environment in which they find themselves, expands, grows, and gets richer and better.

This model of success is what I term "The Success Code", the twelve attributes of a person who has found that hidden treasure that is the object of life on this earth. My appeal to you is that you understand that transformation is a process. In my 30 years of searching, I have not yet found that magic wand which one can just wave and get instant money, instant love, instant employment, and so on. We are living in a fast-paced world in which almost everything needs to be instant, reason why it is *good business* to advertise instant healings, instant prosperity, or instant marriage, be it in churches or success seminars. This book insists on the truth that the journey of the soul is an eternal journey. Like a tree, we must patiently and persistently unfold, germinate, grow, mature, and bear fruit, following the pattern that unfolds naturally in the universe.

It is my promise to you that it is impossible to fail if you commit yourself to study, reflect, and experiment with the intention of making this Success Code become true for you. Every true mystic will tell you that the spiritual journey is a journey that has no destination. In a sense, the destination is the journey itself. Once you are on the right path, life becomes a matter of enjoying the bliss of the journey rather than being distracted by thoughts about arriving at some fixed destination. The practical person will argue that life is about having bread on the table and paying the bills. I will say that he too is right. I will, however, add that if the only thing you came to this world to do was to work a hundred hours a week just to keep up with the bills, and have no time for love, relationship, family, laughter, and doing good in the world, then surely, your god must be crazy.

The Success Code is a pattern for your true life. You alone know where you stand right now with reference to what you *can* be. But I can already tell that if the solution is in working more hours, getting more certificates, trying harder, changing churches, fraternities or political parties, or whatever physical adjustment you can think of, then most of us will require ten life times to fulfill our potential. So, spirituality and practicality are not opposing camps. They are the two sides of the same coin that make up your life. When you find the secret within, and apply it to your outer experience, then your life becomes the miracle it was designed to be.

A code is a program or language that is transcribed or translated into a specific output by an operating system. A software or mobile application is a computer code. The genes in your cells constitute a biological code. Your life is the expression of a subconscious mental code. The Success Code embodies the twelve attributes with which an ideal life can be described, as we have seen in the introduction to this book.

For you to say that you are successful in life, your life must reflect the twelve attributes described in the Success Code above. They are not something you are born with; you cultivate them. And the good news is, there is no one on earth that is so disadvantaged that he/she does not have the means to cultivate these traits. In other words, there is no one who is such a failure that he/she can no longer recreate his/her life into something magnificent that will awe the world. Why? This is because the process is a mental one. The material world only reflects our inner spiritual reality. We cannot change our lives by running around and trying to change outer things. Rather, we need to leave the outer things alone, go within, recreate ourselves the way we want, and then allow the outer world to remodel itself to reflect that which we have created.

As you read through this book, you will experience a power surge similar to what happens when current flows through an electrical device when it is plugged into a main supply. Books of this nature constitute a spiritual vortex through which your life is synced with the Infinite Source of Life. As this Life Force flows through you, it translates your inner state of consciousness into outer experience the same way electricity makes a light bulb to shine. The Force converts into outer manifestation, the stuff you are made of. So, it is imperative to create your ideal life using the Success Code, so that you will have a seed for this Force as you awaken it.

First, you become aware of the fact that there is more to life than you are currently experiencing. Then you come to terms with the promise that your purpose here is not to conform to the standards you came and met, but to find the hidden treasure and let it transform your life. Then you rewire your brain with the image of what your life ought to be. When you visualize the life that could be yours if the Success Code were true for you, it awakens in you the hunger to make it so. A polarity is created; now there is the you that you are now and there is the you that you are becoming. The potential difference between these two extremes becomes the gravitational pull that draws you toward the realization of the better version of you.

CHAPTER 2

The Knight In Us

The second insight;

Within each one of us lies a knight, a genius, a giant, an avatar, a messiah, waiting to be born. What we are born into is a socially constructed hallucination in which we are programmed to sleep-walk through life, not knowing who we truly are and what we came here to do. The moment we wake up from the dream of materiality and recognize that we have been living a lie, the miracle begins to happen. The Christ within us begins to unfold and life starts becoming magical.

Grandpa: *Benjamin Franklin Gates, you take upon yourself the duty of the Templars, the Freemasons and the family Gates. Do you so swear?*
Ben: *I so swear.*

Young Benjamin Franklin Gates has just heard his grandfather narrate to him the most fascinating story of a hidden treasure of unspeakable proportions, and of his ancestors' failed attempts to find the treasure. He has also listened to his father ridicule the idea of a hidden treasure, lamenting the fact that his ancestors were a bunch of fools chasing after fools' gold. According to Patrick Gates, the treasure does not exist. He regrets having wasted twenty years of his own precious life looking for the treasure only to end up with nothing, like his ancestors before him. But Ben cannot fight off the fire that the story has ignited within him. He believes that the treasure is real, and he believes he will find it.

The imagery of the Knights Templar that his grandfather had presented certainly got Ben's attention, for he later asks, "Grandpa, are we knights?". John asks Ben if he wants to be a knight, and Ben nodded in the affirmative. So, John asks him to kneel, and while Ben knelt on the floor, John performs a symbolic knighting ritual.

At face value it seems like the playful interaction between grandfather and grandson. But in reality, on this fateful evening in that dark little attic, a true knight is born.

There is a hero, a messiah, a Christ, a Buddha, an avatar in every one of us. Whether it is Moses, Jesus, Alexander the Great, Napoleon, Gandhi, Luther, or Mandela, history demonstrates that the people who have moved the world did not fall from the sky. They were ordinary people born under ordinary circumstances and living ordinary lives until they experienced their epiphany. Like the Gates family, each of us has come to this world with a special mission to uncover a certain treasure that will enrich humanity.

Like Benjamin Gates, we have all inherited traditional beliefs from our family and environment about who we are, what others before us have tried to do, and what we should not bother to do. Even when we are surrounded by the negative conditioning that tells us that all dreams are a waste of time and that we should just settle down for a little college degree, a decent job, and just enough income to pay the bills, there is always that remnant of prophets – the grandpa who still believes the dream and inspires us to pursue the dream.

The fundamental problem of modern society is that we have a model of success that no longer works, because it is founded on a false premise of the nature of reality, the purpose of life, and our identity as humans. A flawed concept of reality has led us to misinterpret the purpose of life, and this in turn has inspired us to adopt a false identity. Because we are unaware of who we truly are, and what the universe that surrounds us really is, we have reduced our lives to the race for survival that characterizes the beasts in the jungle.

Grandpa Gates represents that voice of inspiration that is calling us to wake up from our hypnotic trance and live the purpose for which we came here. Benjamin Gates is the image of the new generation of awakened souls who despite the noise and haste that surrounds them, have the courage to look within and find that guiding star. The day you awaken from the sleep of the false identity you have been carrying, the darkness of pain, disease, loneliness, poverty, and fear disappear, and the knight resurrects to embrace his noble mission of finding the hidden treasure if life.

The human tragedy is best articulated in the scriptural text from the book of Psalms in the Holy Bible:

"The 'gods' know nothing, they understand nothing. They walk about in darkness; all the foundations of the earth are shaken. "I said, 'You are "gods"; you are all sons of the Most High.' But you will die like mere mortals; you will fall like every other ruler." (Psalm 82:5-7. NIV).

It basically says that we are gods, sons and daughters of the Most High. Yet because of our ignorance of who we are, we walk about in darkness. Jesus makes it clear that this Psalm is referring to all of the human race, and not some particular person:

"Is it not written in your Law, 'I have said you are "gods"'? (John 10:34. NIV).

The foundations of our world are shaky – our education, religion, government, economics, medicine, everything that we have created is shaky, because it is founded on a false premise. And so long as we persist in the false identity and false reality, we will die like mere mortals. Oh, what a tragedy to be born as royalty and yet live the life of a pauper because you are unaware of the fact that you are royalty? What a disgrace to be born as a heavenly prince/princess, yet live and die like an earthworm because you are unaware of the glory that is locked up within you?

You are a privileged being. By virtue of your presence on this planet, you have a right to every good you desire. You have a right to every good thing you need to live all the life you are capable of living. Success, health, love, joy, peace, harmony, prosperity, abundance, and affluence are the natural order of the universe of which you are a part. The world was designed in such a way that every soul that stepped into it would experience more than enough health, more than enough wealth, more than enough love, more than enough happiness, more than enough success, and more than enough prosperity. There is no scarcity of resources in creation. The only problem we have is the problem of uneven distribution, resulting from the wrong philosophies we have been taught about achieving personal success. If you take hold of the right success philosophy and live your life in the light of it, nothing will hinder you from thriving wherever you are.

The fundamental problem of life is that man does not know who he really is. The root of all problems in human society is the fact that human beings are unaware of who they really are. If only you knew who you were, all struggle will cease. The unveiling of the knight within us is the attainment of all things imaginable. There is no secret to success outside of yourself; that which you seek is the True You. When you find the True You, you awaken to the startling recognition that, 'You are the secret'. It is you that is the kingdom of heaven. It is you that is the land of milk and honey.

If human beings become aware of who they really are: work will be transformed from grinding labor to joyful self-expression; relationships will be transformed from tolerance to celebration; business will be transformed from ripping off people for profit, to collaboration in the increase of life for all; physical bodies will be transformed from sick and tired biological machines, to beautiful, buoyant, vibrant, vessels of life; human existence will be transformed from a daily battle for survival, into the blissful, timeless thriving called heaven.

The *False Self-Concept* is the original sin out of which all human suffering emerges. The *True Self-Concept* is the Christ, the Righteousness that we enter into after the second birth or resurrection by which man is enthroned in his rightful place as a son of God. The philosophers of old began their quest with the question, "Who am I?" Jesus of Nazareth tossed the secret to his disciples when he asked, "Who do you say 'I am'?" Self-contemplation is the very definition of spirituality. The day you ask the question "Who am I?" and actively start looking for answers, is the first day you really start living. Without knowing what he was doing, the young and tender Benjamin Gates asked the question that caused the gates of heaven to fly open; "Grandpa are we knights?".

Who do you say you are?

At his request, Ben was symbolically sworn as a knight by his grandfather. Although this was only a symbolic act, young Ben did not know enough to give in to rationalization, doubt, fear, and worry. He was on fire with the desire to find the treasure that had eluded his ancestors. He grew up knowing that he was a knight whose life quest was to find the treasure. This sense of identity and purpose determined the choices he made about what fields of study and work to engage in, and ultimately drew the blueprint of his life. This is the secret hidden within this scene of the *National Treasure* movie: your sense of identity determines your purpose, your sense of purpose determines your beliefs, your beliefs govern your choices, and your choices ultimately define your reality. The Ultimate philosophical law of life is "man know thyself", and it has been voiced by the great philosophers that "the unexamined life is not worth living". Thus, it is not only fitting but imperative to begin your new journey with the question "Who am I?" No matter who you are, where you are, what you have, and how old you may be, it is the day you ask this question that you stop existing and start living for the first time.

Is your name your identity?

If you ask me who I am, and I respond that I am Godfrey, it doesn't take much effort to realize that the name Godfrey is not who I really am. I will still be the same me if I was called by another name. Many people allow their existence to be limited by the name by which they are called. Some people are named after their relatives; others after a notable figure, sports or entertainment star, or movie character; others are named after a saint; others still are named after a memorable event in the lives of their parents; and there are people who have the names they have for just no reason.

Because of the popular culture that names have meaning, we subconsciously define ourselves by the assumed meaning behind our names and often get stuck in that definition. The good news is that your name is not who you are. When a person undertakes a name change, he has to make a certificate for that name change because his face does not change. Not even a hair on your head will fall off or change its color if you change your name from 'Franka Brown' to 'Ayuk'. You are not your name – you have a name.

So, who is the You that has that name? By recognizing that "I am not the name by which I am called", we have unmasked the first false identity. *Your name is not your true identity.*

Is your age your identity?

I am now 37 years old, so what? The biological clock by which your physical life experience evolves is not the real you. Once upon a time you were one second old, then you became 1 year old, then you became 10 years old, 20 years old, and now 36 years old. The clock will continue ticking to 50, 60, 70, 80, and maybe 90. Ultimately you will move beyond the clock, just as you came from beyond the clock. You came out of some unknown zone that is beyond time, to experience life on this space-time dimension, and then exit back into the unknown zone.

If you were really your age, it wouldn't have been possible to experience yourself as a baby, an infant, a teenager, an adult, a senior, and still be the same you. So, if your age is not your identity, who is it that is having these ages? By recognizing that "I am not my age", we have unmasked the second false identity.

This is a liberating experience because now you can stand apart from the age you identify with, observe yourself, and freely choose the life you want to experience, despite what your birth certificate says. *Your age is not your true identity.*

Is your body your identity?

Are you your body? You are used to saying my body, my arm, my head, my leg, etc., in the same way you say my house, my clothes, my car, etc. This is because it is not the body talking about itself, but rather a self that is talking about the body as an experience it is having. The body you had when you were five years old no longer exists. The body you have now will not exist five years from now. As you read these words billions of cells in your body are being replaced by new ones. The lifespan of a red blood cell is 72 days. What that means is that the red blood cells that are transporting the oxygen you are breathing in today and supplying it to all the cells of your body, will not be alive in the next three months.

In the same way, each cell in your body has a lifespan, after which it is replaced by completely new cells. Biologists estimate that your body has a turn-over time of two years. That is, within two years from today, almost every cell that is in your body now will have been replaced by a new one. So, you cannot be your body because your body itself is a very fluid existence.

If we have found that the "I" is not the body, then we have unmasked the third false identity. We must, therefore, continue our search into the deeper layers of being. *You are not your body.*

Is your gender your identity?

When you say, "I am a male", "I am a female", it is clear that it is not male or female speaking. There is someone else describing himself as male or herself as female. We know in developmental biology that at the early stages of life, the embryo has no gender. A process called 'sex differentiation' actually occurs somewhere along the developmental process in response to the genetics that has been inherited by the fetus under formation.

Now, if life is present before sex differentiation, what gender is that life? We are forced to return to the biblical statement in Matthew 22:30 that in heaven there is no taking of wives (because in heaven there is neither male nor female). So, on the journey to look for our identity, we find that gender is not the final bus stop.

Imagine the implication this simple awareness can have on human society. The gender discrimination that has permeated our religions, cultures, governments, and work places for centuries suddenly vanishes into nothingness when we realize that it is based on a false assumption. *The gender is not the real self.*

Is your tribe your identity?

On our imaginary space travel in search of the True Self, we arrive at the planet called Tribe, and we ask the question, "Am I the tribe I come from?" If you come from those parts of Africa, Asia, South America or the Middle East where traditional societies are still very strong, you will easily grasp the concept of tribe. But do not be surprised that the average kid in New York or London does not know what a tribe is. A tribe in its original definition means *a social group in a traditional society consisting of families or communities linked by social, economic, religious, or blood ties, with a common culture and dialect, and typically having a recognized leader.*

Globalization has engendered the progressive mingling and dilution of tribes. It is common to find an American of Japanese origin who has never been to Japan, cannot speak the local dialect of his people, and in fact is oblivious of the existence of the tribe of his ancestors. Apart from the Native Indian Americans, every other American is an immigrant. The only difference between one and the other is how far back your ancestors stepped foot on the New World.

While the concept of tribe may not be very relevant in the developed world, tribalism is the root of untold evil in other parts of the world. Genocides have been committed because of tribal identification, governments are formed and the resources of countries are partitioned to favor people based on their tribes, people experience discrimination and mockery because of their tribal history, dialect or culture, and intertribal wars continue to be the cause of loss of lives and property on a daily basis.

If your grandfather came from Poland, married a woman from Mexico who gave birth to your mother who later married a man from Africa and gave birth to you, and you have never been to Europe, Mexico, or Africa, where would you say your tribe is? The truth is that your tribe practically does not exist in your experience. So, if it is possible for you to exist outside your tribe, could we conclude satisfactorily that your tribe is not your true identity? Now, we have unmasked the fifth false identity by finding out that "I am not my tribe". *The tribe is not the true self.*

Is your race your identity?

Is Black African your identity? Is Hispanic your identity? Is Caucasian your identity? Is Asian your identity? If your identity was defined by the color of your skin, hair, or eyes, the shape of your nose and your sensitivity to ultraviolet rays, what identity does a child have whose father is black and the mother is Asian? What identity will this child's child have if he marries a Hispanic?

Identity implies something constant, permanent, unchanging. But human evolution has proven that race is like paint. We can mix genes in any combinations over as many generations as human interactions allow. The way you look is called a phenotype. It is coded by your genes. To say that you are your race implies that you are your genetic make-up. But genetics is just a bunch of biological codes that are dead in themselves in the absence of an intelligence to read and express them.

When a person dies the genes remain and disintegrate with the body. So, except you are one of those who believe that man is just a biological robot who ceases to be, at the instance called death, you will agree that beyond your looks, and beyond the genes coding for your looks, there is something else. If this is true then we come to the conclusion that "I am not my race".

Thanks to the marvelous breakthroughs in medical science "Ancestry DNA" testing is becoming more and more fashionable in America. What I find interesting about Ancestry DNA test results is that it is very difficult to find any human being alive today in the modern world who is a so-called 'pure breed', The average person is a mix of races. If you do your Ancestry DNA the result will be presented in percentages of various ancestral genes, meaning that the face you have now simply reveals which of those genes is dominant in the mix. Whether you like it or not, all human races may be flowing in your bloodstream right now. *Race is not your true identity.*

This simple realization is enough to heal the wounds of the two greatest evils ever recorded in human history: the holocaust in Europe, and slavery in America.

Is your social image your identity?

Are you a doctor or teacher? Did you graduate from Harvard or Buea? Are you an Army General or Buddhist Monk? Take a close look at the decorations that you have amassed. Usually, your resumé (curriculum vitae) and the certificates, medals, and photos on your wall are the best help for such an exercise.

Social image is what most of us live for, and the bigger and more influential the image, the more fulfilled we feel. But look again. Are you this social image? Would you cease to be you if you were a shoe mender instead of an engineer? Would you cease to be you if you were a catechist instead of a diplomat? Would you cease to be you if you were a village housewife instead of the Queen of England?

The idea of an image is that it is a perception of yourself that you are projecting to the world. Who then is it that is projecting and observing this image? There must be someone beyond, that is creating and experiencing himself/herself as this image. You can be president today, and a normal husband and father tomorrow, like Obama. You can be a cardinal today and a prisoner tomorrow. What the world thinks of you and what you know about yourself when you lie on your bed at night, are they the same thing? *Surely, your social image is not your identity.*

Is your intellect your identity?

Your intellect is your logical reasoning mind. Your intellect is the activity of the brain, the sea of ideas and images that you generate as you experience life. Every action is preceded by an idea. You have the idea of moving your finger and your muscles respond to that idea and make the finger move. You have the idea of eating a sandwich and your body mechanism responds by triggering the cascade of chemical reactions, nerve impulses and muscle movements that culminate in you eating that sandwich.

How many thoughts do you think you have in a single day? Neuroscientists tell us that the average human brain weighs 3pounds, contains about 100 billion brain cells (neurons), and receives a blood supply of 750-1000mls of blood per minute. It is estimated that the average person thinks 50,000 – 70,000 thoughts a day, and between 40% – 50% of total body heat is lost through the head (through brain activity).

This miracle of nature called the brain is so fascinating that we will not be punished for thinking that the "I" must be located inside the brain. But let us see; if you were to take the brain outside the body, will it stay alive and continue to think? If the answer is no, then there must be someone else that is thinking with the brain, seeing with the eye, hearing with the ear, smelling with the nose, tasting with the tongue, and touching with the skin.

Therefore, the conscious mind (the brain and all the senses that serve it) is not the self and the self is not found inside the brain. *You are not your intellect.*

Are your beliefs your identity?

Beliefs are patterns of thought that have been programmed into your subconscious self like software. Your thoughts, feelings, words, and actions flow spontaneously from your beliefs the same way the physical characteristics of your body flow spontaneously from your genes. Your religion, political opinion, scientific or cultural inclinations, and your habitual lifestyle, constitute pronounced manifestations of your belief system. Habits are patterns of action that we have programmed into our body through repeated action, to the degree that as far as those actions are concerned, the body has become the mind or control center.

We notice every day that a Republican can change his mind and become a Democrat simply because he does not like the person occupying the White House. A Roman Catholic can become a Protestant simply because he has married someone from the other denomination. The same person who is a chronic alcoholic today can be tomorrow the soberest fellow on the block. Such swings in opinion or habits are an indication that a belief is simply a program that one writes in his consciousness, and this program can always be replaced by another program as the need arises. A stronger belief or habit will always overwrite a weaker belief or habit.

Now, when we talk of a program we immediately think of the programmer. If there is a programmer, then clearly the belief, the program, is not the real self. And with this observation, we conclude that the belief system is not the "I" that we are in search of. Your religion is not your identity; your political party is not your identity; your cult is not your identity; your addiction is not your identity. All these are experiences you are having. Therefore, by detaching from them and finding the true self, you can be free from them. *You are not your beliefs.*

Is your Soul the real you?

Pushing our frontier further, we arrive at the soul. Oh, at last, maybe we have found it! The soul is the container of our beliefs or subjective conditioning. It has been called the heart (not the physical heart), or the sub-conscious mind. It has been credited with the power of creating our outer reality. Psychologists tell us that the soul or sub-conscious mind is the place where the individual consciousness mingles with the Infinite Consciousness. So, it is through the soul that man has access to the Spiritual Realm. Therefore, the soul must be the "I".

Or maybe not! Right now, as you read these words, there is someone observing the soul as though he were apart from it. There is someone who has traveled through these levels of self-identification in search of the self; from the name, the age, the gender, the tribe, the race, the body, the image, the intellect, the beliefs, and now has arrived at the soul. The soul appears to be a vessel in which that someone programs the patterns or codes that get spontaneously expressed as your experiences. It appears that the soul is a hard drive, the beliefs are the program, and experience is the output. Where then are the programmer and the operating system? So, we find that even the soul is not the "I".

At the end of our futile search for the self in our experiences, we now turn to the only place that is left for us to turn to. Who is it that has been making this observation? Who is it that has been journeying through the layers of self-identification in search of the self? Who is it that boarded that imaginary spacecraft at the beginning of this exercise and navigated the various human experiences in search of the self? It was the True Self. We, therefore, come to the awakening, the point of realization that the True Self is not the name, the age, the gender, the tribe, the race, the image, the body, the intellect, or the soul. These are experiences that the Self is having. These experiences are contained within the Self. If this is true then we have proven that the Self is immaterial, the Self is a conscious entity, the Self is beyond space and time, the Self precedes birth and supersedes death.

We have found the Self to be that which is consciousness or spirit, creates its experiences through the awareness of itself, is beyond space and time, and transcends birth and death. Now we say that God is the Infinite Spirit that creates and experiences the universe through the awareness of Himself, is beyond space and time, and transcends birth and death (is not created and cannot be destroyed). The Self we have found in us is identical to the God we find in the universe. Therefore, we can safely conclude that the Self, the True Identity of man, is the Individualization of the Infinite. We have arrived at this conclusion using a scientific approach, so that when next you read in your scripture that, "You are gods, all of you are sons of the Most High", you should not have any doubt about it anymore.

We have found the Father, the God of the universe to be the Father in us who is living and moving and having His Being in us, through us, and as us. We have found the universal "I AM" to be identical to the "I am" in us. Each time you say, "I am", it is God that is saying "I AM" through you, thus we come to the realization that Moses had in the burning bush when God revealed Himself to him as "I am that I AM" (Exodus 3:14). We come to the reality that Jesus revealed when he said: "I and the Father are one" (John 10:30). We come to the realization that Paul had when he said: "It is not I that lives, but Christ living through me" (Galatian 2:20). This is the experience of illumination, the new birth by which we have become heirs of God. This is the experience of Transformation, the birth of the knight in us.

CHAPTER 3

The Meaning of Good and Evil

The third insight:

Good and evil are not opposites. They are the two sides of the coin of life. Just as we cannot appreciate the light without the background darkness, evil is the contrast against which the good erupts and is experienced. Whatsoever is negative in our life is there to point us to its contrast that we are desiring to experience. Rather than fight the negative, our job is to intend its opposite and pursue it.

Thirty years have gone by. Ben is now a historian, cryptologist, and treasure hunter. His research has led him to the discovery that the secret that his grandfather had passed on to him is making reference to "The Charlotte", a ship that was lost in the Arctic and buried in ice several years ago. Ben organizes an expedition with Ian Howe, and his friend, Riley Poole, a computer expert, to find The Charlotte.

When they find The Charlotte, there is no treasure in it. It is an old frail ship laden with human skeletons, barrels of gunpowder and other worthless items. They are visibly disappointed. Then they come upon a Meerschaum Pipe which has a clue on it. Ben's interpretation of the clue reveals that the next clue is hidden behind the most important document in America - the Declaration of Independence.

When Ian suggests they steal the Declaration of Independence, Ben opposes the idea.

Ian: Look, Ben... I understand your bitterness. I really do. You've spent your entire life searching for this treasure, only to have the respected historical community treat you and your family with mockery and contempt. You should be able to rub this treasure in their arrogant faces, and I want you to have the chance to do that.

Ian does not succeed to convince Ben to give in to the idea of breaking into the National Archives and stealing the Declaration of Independence. Ian decides that if Ben is not going to partner with him to rob the National Archives, then he will be better off if Ben is not alive to stop him. A fight ensues between them resulting in a massive fire fueled by gunpowder, and the group split in two. Ian and his men escape the burning ship while Ben and Riley take cover just before the ship explodes.

Ben, Ian, and Riley are one team. They have worked together for quite a while and seem to be quite close. Ben and Riley are friends. Ben and Ian play poker together. So, the relationship between the three goes beyond just work and the treasure hunt. The clue "The secret lies with Charlotte" has led them to an old ship named Charlotte that had been lost at sea several years before and thanks to Riley's computer models, they had located it trapped under the ice in the Arctic. The team is excited about finding the treasure, only to be disappointed that they have come this far just to find another clue.

But it is a clue that is unusual. If Ben's interpretation is correct, then the next clue is an invisible map hidden on the back of the Declaration of Independence. Breaking into the National Archives and stealing a national monument as important as the Declaration of Independence is certainly not the kind of adventure Ben is carved out for. This is where the difference between Ben and Ian becomes apparent. Ben is a genuine scholar who is hunting the treasure for a motive quite different from that of Ian who will do anything to lay his hands on it. In the midst of the argument between Ben and Ian, Ian orders Shaw to pull a gun, Ben lights a flare, the result is that the ship that is loaded with gunpowder goes up in a massive explosion and two opposing teams emerge – Ben and Riley are the good guys, while Ian and his team are the bad guys.

This scene portrays the classic birth of duality. While philosophers and theologians have spent millennia trying to explain why evil exists, all schools of thought agree that life is a pulsating phenomenon that occurs between two poles: the Absolute Good and its opposite, the Absolute Evil. In between these two extremes we find that life is a spiral of levels of being that ascends from the lowest level of evil to the highest level of good.

Religion personifies the Absolute Good as God and the Absolute Evil as Satan. When we take a closer look, we realize that there is really no such thing as a purely good thing or person, or a purely bad thing or person. Every reality contains in itself the duality and is what it is by virtue of its position on the scale. Using the temperature scale as an analogy, we find that an object at 50°C is hot in relation to an object at 0 °C and cold in relation to an object at 100 °C.

Duality is the fundamental law of the universe that lays the foundation for the mechanics through which life evolves. The primary duality of good and evil is manifested on the material universe as the various universal laws of polarity, cause and effect, male and female, positive and negative, above and below, within and without, rhythm, etc. In mathematics, two lines that appear parallel must meet somewhere if they are extrapolated to infinity. In physics, all force fields must converge within a certain unified field.

In spirituality, all things emerge from and return to the One Source or Creator. Having this background in mind helps us move away from the human tendency to judge and label people and things as good or bad, labels that condition our responses and interactions with the world around us. When we understand what is going on, we realize that each person, thing, or event is here to play its designated part in the drama of life, whose purpose is to help us find and achieve our purpose. Light can only be perceived in the background of darkness. Therefore, in order for us to experiences the goodness that we are in essence, we must have a playground of contrast, that which we call evil.

In the Bible, the birth of duality is depicted in the metaphor of the "Fall of Man" in the Garden of Eden. To begin with, it will be helpful to bear in mind that the creation story of Genesis is not a historical account of how God actually created the world and how an actual Adam and Eve committed an actual original sin by obeying an actual serpent and eating an actual forbidden fruit. The Genesis account of creation is a myth written by Hebrew mystics using the language and symbols that were part of their spiritual tradition at the time.

A myth is a traditional story, legend, or folklore, weaved by a culture to convey an underlying deeper message such as the origin of life, natural and social phenomena, etc., without the story itself needing to be true. Myths, allegories, metaphors, proverbs, and parables, constituted the standard mode of teaching among the philosophers and spiritual masters of old, and are still widely used in the indigenous traditions of Africa.

The problem of life is that we have accepted duality as the fact of life rather than a phenomenon of life. In so doing we have created a dichotomy between man and God. We have engraved in our consciousness the paradigm that man is inherently evil and that the purpose of life is to seek salvation from evil and earn an eternal reward from the God we have fabricated and enthroned in some far-off heaven. This dualist concept of reality is the basis of religion. Because of its flawed premise, most religious doctrines about man, God, laws, sacraments, and worship are severely limited. Religion depicts man as a miserable, worthless, mortal creature, who is inherently sinful and destined to hell, unless he subscribes to a set of religious creeds and rituals, claimed to have been handed down by a God who will reward those who obey him and punish those who do not.

One does not need philosophical arguments to expose the fact that the image that the major religions paint of God is exactly that of the kings of old. Our ancestors simply took the ancient concept of a kingdom, a supreme king, the king's (right) hand, the subjects, the rewards of the loyal and the punishment of the disloyal citizens. They then amplified this model of thought to the concept of a celestial kingdom, and in the process, created God in the image of man. It is only when we transcend the zone of duality and view life from the vantage point of unity from which the duality emerges that we can find the truth of our being.

There are two mechanisms through which beliefs are formed:

Default programming

From conception, through childhood, we are programmed by the dominant thought patterns of our ancestry, culture, parentage, education, religion, and social interactions. This default programming happens without us being aware of it, and we grow up being, not our authentic selves, but a generic expression of the environment we grow up in. So long as our life is running on the default conditioning, we do not have free will. This is because it is not us making the choices but the program choosing for us. It is not us reacting to the environment, but the program reacting to the environment. And since it is not us that wrote and installed the program, we cannot claim that we are truly living. It is the environment that is living itself through us. Our routines, habits, personality traits, and addictions can testify to this.

A careful observation will reveal that 95% of the daily activities of the average person are automatic. That is, they are unconscious. You wake up every morning on the exact side of the bed, put on your slippers in the exact way, walk to the bathroom and brush your teeth without thinking, make and eat your breakfast, bathe, get dressed, get to work, do your job, and return home. Your life is so predictable that it can be programmed as a computer simulation and the simulation will work with about 95% accuracy.

Deliberate programming

From the moment we become aware of the game that is going on, we recognize that the self-concept we have been carrying is false, and hence all our experiences have been faulty. By recognizing the false as false, we awaken to the deeper truth that lies behind the mask of conditioning, and find that this truth is our Authentic Self, the Christ, the Spirit of the universe living in us, as us, and through us. When our being becomes centered on this Spirit within instead of the evidence of the senses, we begin to freely recreate our personal reality. Deliberate programming is done through your contemplation of the attributes that are manifest in the universe. That which you contemplate the universe as, and accept as true for you, you program into your new belief system.

When the new program reaches the threshold where it overwrites the old program, then a transformation takes place. If you are given an unlimited amount of clean water and you start pouring it into a bucket of dirty water, the clean water consistently dilutes the dirty water till you reach the point where there is only clean water left. This is the mechanism of mental transmutation. This explains why the same treatment will work for one patient and not for another with the same condition, and why two people with the same condition will attend a healing service and one will get a healing miracle while the other stays the same. The density of subconscious conditioning determines the intensity and duration of exposure to Truth before the critical moment of transformation is attained.

It is impossible to alter a belief while functioning within the same self-concept that created the belief. You cannot enter the kingdom of heaven unless you are born again. In order to be born again, you must die to the old self. All religious doctrines, success philosophies, as well as social ethics, norms and moral codes that are based on the manipulation of the mind and its beliefs, or the use of effort to alter circumstances, end up being part of the problem rather than the cure.

No amount of positive thinking, affirmations, and physical formulas will change the content of your subconscious mind unless you first adopt a higher self-concept. The ultimate self-concept is the realization that "I and the Father are One". This is the Christ Awareness. The Christ Awareness opens up the inner eye of intuition to behold the universe as the spontaneous unfolding of Infinite Life, Love, Beauty, Wisdom, Power, Harmony, and Abundance. As the awakened being contemplates this as the reality of the universe with which he is one, he inadvertently mirrors these qualities in himself. And gradually the point comes when you break loose from all resistance and attain the state of free fall. This is where you walk in miracles as naturally as the leaves cover the tree.

The "I" or the "Self" is an unconditioned Intelligence, or Pure Consciousness that exists beyond space and time, and experiences itself as that which it identifies itself as. When the Self identifies itself as a soul, it experiences itself as a soul. When the Self identifies itself as a set of beliefs, it experiences itself as those beliefs. When the Self identifies itself as the intellect, it experiences itself as the intellect. When the Self identifies itself as the body, it experiences itself as the body. When the Self identifies itself as the social image, it experiences itself as the social image. When the Self identifies itself with the gender, it experiences itself as the gender. When the Self identifies itself as the age, it experiences itself as the age. When the Self identifies itself as the race, it experiences itself as the race. When the Self identifies itself as the name, it experiences itself as the name. The Self does not have these experiences on the sequential scale with which we have examined them. The Self exists beyond space and time, meaning that it is having all these experiences simultaneously. All that exists, exists within the Self.

Each time you peel off a layer of conditioning through the recognition that that conditioning is not the Self, you set your life free from the limited experiences that have been created as a result of your identification with that conditioning (your assuming a false identity). When you ultimately arrive at the true nature of the Self, your True Identity or Authentic Self, you have died to the old self and experienced the new birth. It is true what scripture says, "no one can enter the kingdom of heaven unless he is born again". If heaven is that state characterized by the highest ideal of existence, then it is pretty obvious that man cannot attain his highest potential by fixing or improving the old self. Like the grain of wheat falls to the ground and dies, you must die to the false self, in order for the new and true self to emerge.

That which is beyond time and space, is permanent and unchanging, has life in itself, and transcends the phenomena called birth, growth, and death, fits the description of what we call God. If the "I" that we have found to be the true you, is characterized by these God-like qualities, then haven't we proven scientifically that man is the image of God, that we are all gods and sons of the Most High? The "I", the "Self", the "True Identity of man", is God Eternal living and moving and having His being in human form. God is in the process of experiencing Himself as human - you; therefore, you are right now a god, a child of the Most High. The degree to which you identify with conditions or experiences determines how far you fall from grace into the state called sin, evil, or death. The degree to which you are aware of your divine identity and observe your experiences as mere experiences, determines the degree to which you rise in goodness and glory.

Man is an individualized consciousness living and moving and having his being within an Infinite Consciousness that is living and moving and having Its Being in, through, and as man. If reality can be likened to an ocean, then man would be a drop in that ocean. The drop and the ocean are one and indivisible. The ocean is the drop and the drop is the ocean. Consciousness, in the process of being aware of itself as Infinity, is Pure Consciousness, Pure Being or Pure Potentiality. Consciousness in the process of being aware of itself as individuality is Individualized Consciousness or Man. Pure Consciousness is referred to in Scripture as the Father and Individualized Consciousness is referred to as the Son. And we are told that "the Father is in me and I am in the Father...he who sees me sees the Father...I and the Father are one".

If Infinite Consciousness is the ultimate reality and man is the individualization of Infinite Consciousness, then the purpose of individualization, the reason why God becomes man, is to create the mirror of relationship through which self-experience can take place. In your personal life, it is pretty clear to you that you cannot experience who you are, except in relation to something else. The Son is the Image of the Father, projected by the Father within Himself, through which the Father can contemplate and experience Himself. It is therefore through the Son that the Father glorifies himself.

Thus, we can clearly establish that the law governing human life can be nothing else but the spontaneous, unconditional and perpetual outpouring of the Infinite Life of the Father into and through the Son – that which we have found to be the true identity of man. This spontaneous, unconditional and perpetual outpouring of Infinite Consciousness into expression in, through, and as individual consciousness is the Life Force we call Love, Grace, The Breath of God, The Word of God, the Will of God, Divine Intention, or the Holy Spirit. It is out of death that life emerges; It is in the midst of sin that grace abounds; good and evil are not opposites, they are the complementary pair that creates the environment within which experience unfolds.

Adam is the human being whose awareness is limited to the world of his senses. He is said to have fallen into ego-consciousness because his self-awareness is trapped in the world of external phenomena. He believes himself to be the ego and sees his external world to be his reality. By knowing the external world to be his reality he is entranced in the contemplation of the external world, thereby recreating it in his reality. All his efforts are directed toward reacting to, fighting against, or trying to fix the external reality. But the more he gives his energy to the external, the more he reinforces this false concept of self. He is thus in a state of perpetual sin and his only salvation is to die. Ian and his quest to acquire the treasure at all cost and use it for personal aggrandizement, is the image of Adam or evil in our National Treasure movie.

Jesus of Nazareth appears as the second Adam. He embodies the Adam nature as a human being but fulfills the condition for entering the new kingdom; he dies to the Adam Self and Resurrects as the Christ Self. Thus, the real miracle of the universe is not Christmas but Easter. It is the resurrection that constitutes the second birth. The transformative experience is the death of the ego-self or human nature so that the Christ Self or Divine Nature may resurrect in its place. When we become these transformed Beings, we find that blessedness is our natural state of being, miracles are natural occurrences in our daily lives, and heaven is our natural atmosphere.

The story of the fall of Adam is not the fascinating drama of an actual man called Adam who ate a certain fruit in an actual Garden of Eden thereby committing the original sin that all humanity has inherited. It is a metaphor that explains the primitive state of consciousness of incarnate man as he first appears on earth. The story of the birth, death, and resurrection of Jesus is the real-life exemplification of the second birth that every human being is destined to experience. Every seed is destined to germinate and give form to the tree it contains.

Man is God-in-embryo and his destiny is to germinate (through the death of the old self) and give manifestation to the divine life that is contained within him. Jesus is Master, Messiah, and Savior because he is the archetype of the human experience. Building a religion around him may be helpful, but it is not necessary. The invitation is not to sit at morning Mass every day and profess the Apostles' Creed or attend the healing services of some fantastic prophet. The invitation of life is for every one of us to replicate in our lives, the mystery that is revealed through Christ Jesus; the mystery of our oneness with the Father, and the Father's glory overflowing through us.

The death of the human identity or *false self-concept* occurs when you recognize the falsity of it. You recognize the falsity of the human identity by the contemplative process of examining this accumulation of conditionings that make up your subconscious mind and how they came about. By detaching from them, examining them, and proving to yourself through logical reasoning that they are false, they simply disappear like darkness gives way to light. That which you have proven to yourself through logical reason you automatically accept as fact. You do not need the laborious process of trying to believe them against your reason. You do not need the stress of affirming them over and over until your mind has been fooled into accepting them as true. You do not need to fast and pray about them and hope that God will change things for you.

That which you know through evidence, becomes a direct experience, and this is what is known as Faith. Faith makes you invincible. Have you ever asked why Saul of Tarsus who was never a disciple of Jesus, who after the death and resurrection of Jesus got converted into the Apostle Paul, turned out to be the most valuable apostle, his writings accounting for over half of the New Testament? His secret is contained in his own words found in Galatians 1:15-16 (KJV),

"But when it pleased God, who separated me from my mother's womb, and called me by his grace, to reveal his Son in me, that I might preach him among the heathen; immediately I conferred not with flesh and blood."

The transformative experience is the state of conviction you enter into where you know that this Son, this Christ, this Father in me, this I AM, is the Truth that you call your "I am". To awaken to your *True Self-concept* is to have become the risen Christ. When this miracle occurs, you will not ask for advice, permission, or validation from any outside authority.

You can become a transformed being while yet in a difficult relationship, even a divorce process. You can become a transformed being while yet unemployed and homeless. You can become a transformed being while yet battling with addiction or identity crises. You can become a transformed being while yet battling with grieve over a loved one, drowning in guilt, contemplating suicide, or simply wondering what the hell you are doing on this planet. It doesn't matter if you are Lucifer's chief of staff. The whole point of the Transformative message is that no matter who you are, no matter where you are, no matter what religious or scientific dogma you have been following, no matter your political opinion or other social conditionings, when the sun rises, it doesn't ask permission from the darkness.

All that is negative in your life will progressively fade away as you enter into this light and stay in it. And in their place will appear the atmosphere of miracles you have been yearning for. The Transformative experience is dramatized for us in the Bible as the promised land where we will drink from wells we did not dig, harvest from fields where we did not sow, and drink wine from grapes we did not plant.

The message here is that when you become a transformed being, you are translated into a plane of existence that is governed by laws higher than the physical laws. Since it is a law of nature that the lower laws always serve the higher laws, everything on the material plane will thus exist for the sole purpose of serving you.

CHAPTER 4

Tradition and The Illusion of Security

The fourth insight:

We are all products of conditioning. Our genetics and environment have programmed into our subconscious minds the belief system or paradigm from which we think, feel, speak, act, and interact with the world. The paradigm is the lens through which we perceive the world, and the conditioner of our automatic responses. For the most part we are sleep-walking through life because more than 95% of our activities are spontaneous expressions of our subconscious programming. Our conditioned reality is the comfort zone in which we live most of our lives. Because we are not aware of what is going on, we have no desire for change, and most times we even resist change.

Ben and Riley return to Washington D.C. and report the potential theft of the Declaration to the Federal Bureau of Investigation (FBI) and Dr. Abigail Chase of the National Archives. Both the FBI and Abigail dismiss their claim.

The FBI, and the Department of Homeland Security cannot possibly believe that someone can actually break in and steal the Declaration of Independence. It is one of the most protected documents in the world. Ben must be out of his mind. His claim must be one of the false alarms that the FBI receives on a daily basis.

Ben assumes a false name, Brown, and books an audience with Doctor Abigail Chase of the National Archives.

Abigail: You told my assistant that this was an urgent matter?
Ben: Yes, ma'am. Well, I'm gonna get straight to the point. Someone's gonna steal the Declaration of Independence.
Abigail: I think I'd better put you gentlemen in touch with the FBI...
Ben: We've been to the FBI.
Abigail: And...?
Riley: They assured us that the Declaration cannot possibly be stolen.
Abigail: They're right.

With the hope that Abigail will better understand what he is talking about since she is an expert in the field, Ben opens up to her about the invisible map hidden at the back of the Declaration, which his latest clue had pointed to. The idea of an invisible treasure map sounds ridiculous to a conventional academic mind like Abigail.

Abigail: A treasure map?
Riley: That's where we lost the FBI.
Abigail: You're treasure hunters, aren't you?
Ben: We're more like treasure protectors.
Abigail: Mr. Brown, I have personally seen the back of the Declaration of Independence, and I promise you the only

thing there is a notation that reads, "Original Declaration of Independence", dated...
Ben: *July 4, 1776, yes, ma'am.*
Abigail: *But no map.*
Ben: *It's invisible.*
Abigail:*[sarcastically] Oh, right.*
Riley: *And that's where we lost the Department of Homeland Security.*

The FBI is certain that the Declaration of Independence cannot be stolen. It is not even worth thinking about. The Department of Homeland Security thinks so too. The director of the National Archives thinks it's a laughing issue. The Declaration document is safe within the impenetrable walls of the National Archives and guarded by digital sensors that work to perfection. No one can steal the Declaration of Independence. Or so they think. Riley presents Ben with an excellent analysis of the impossibility.

Riley: *OK Ben. Pay attention. I've brought you to the Library of Congress. Why? Because it's the biggest library in the world. Over twenty million books, and they're all saying the same exact thing: listen to Riley. What we have here is an entire layout of the Archives: sort of builder's blueprints. We've got construction manuals, phone lines, water and sewage. It's all right here... Now, when the Declaration is on display, it is surrounded by guards...and video monitors... and little families from Iowa... and little kids on their eighth grade field trip. And underneath an inch of bulletproof glass is an army of sensors and heat monitors if someone gets too close with a high fever. Now, when it's not on display, it is lowered into a four foot thick concrete, steel-plated vault that happens to be equipped with an electronic combination lock and biometric access-denial systems.*

The world in which we live has a personality of its own. The collective unconscious constitutes the soul of the universe. All the mental energy that has been infused into the universe by all the souls that have been here before us, combined with all the mental energies of all the people in the world, constitute the mental atmosphere in which we live as conscious beings. Every soul that is incarnated into the world inherits the collective unconscious of the human race as a whole, plus the collective unconscious of the race, tribe, and family into which it is born. Within the first seven years of life, the further programming that the child receives from the family, school, church, and environment interact with the inherited program to shape and seal that which becomes the personality. The concept of original sin and the need for baptism therefore has a philosophical basis, although the way the churches go about it does not necessarily makes sense.

The default paradigm or personality is set by the time we are seven, and the tragedy for most people is that even though they live up to seventy, they are simply playing out this default program. The message of this book is that your default self is not who you truly are, but rather, the seed out of which your sublime self is to be born, and that the purpose of life is to give birth to this sublime self and let it illuminate the world.

Man is a conscious being who creates his experiences through the process of self-reflection. His thoughts are a movement of awareness between his self-concept (that which he calls "I") and his environment. Your self-concept determines how you respond to your environmental triggers, and the accumulation of responses builds patterns or subconscious highways that your future actions automatically follow. These subconscious patterns are called beliefs. Before his spiritual awakening, man is a product of his beliefs because he is unaware of the conditioning process that takes place from his conception till adulthood, and further on till he breaks the chain through awareness. Your controlling beliefs are the gods you have enthroned in your life by recognizing them has having causative power over you.

When you belief that a certain force has the power to affect your life, you have given your power to that force through your process of belief. You have made it a god over you. In this chapter, we will examine the stages through which man has evolved as a conscious being and what mental conditionings have brought us to the place where we are today. The importance of this exercise is that by becoming aware of the existence of these forces and understanding their true nature, you free yourself from the grip they have had over your life and enjoy the liberty of rewriting the subconscious script from which your life is played.

Self-concept + Environmental triggers = Beliefs

False Self-concept + Environmental triggers = Limiting Beliefs; hence a burdened life.

True Self-concept + Environmental triggers = Empowering Beliefs; hence a blissful life.

Subconscious conditioning through Fear

Fear can be traced back as the first step in man's conscious evolution. When man first stepped foot on this planet, he was totally ignorant of who he was, what his purpose on the planet was, what the nature of the forces that surrounded him was, and what his relationship with his environment was. The birth of self-awareness or the ego meant the creation of the curtain of separation between the self, and the rest of reality. The survival instinct was born by which primitive man responded to any stimulus by the emotion of fright. Depending on the perceived danger to his survival, he responded to this stimulus in one of two ways; fight or flight.

This primitive state of consciousness is still the dominant state of most humans today. The stock market, the government, the taxman, the landlord, our jobs, the terrorists, even our spouses have become the modern-day predators. Even our religions are based on fear, for the reason that we go to churches, mosques, temples or synagogues more out of fear of eternal punishment from the God who gave us laws to obey, than out of the conviction of our own divinity and the joy of celebrating the life in us. Stress is the greatest epidemic to ever befall humanity, and it is no wonder that most medical conditions are stress related. To unlock the secret of life that is found within us, we must understand and transcend this primitive level of consciousness called *fear.*

Subconscious conditioning through <u>Chance</u>

Early man relied on chance for his survival. When he came upon a fruit that looked good to the eye, he tasted it. If it tasted good, then he ate it. When the season was such that there were no fruits and vegetables, in order not to die of hunger, it dawned on him that he could kill a smaller animal and eat. The capacity for intention or the exercise of free will or volition was absent because he had not gathered enough experience to be able to create mental patterns of cause and effect. Driven by the need to survive, man made use of anything that came his way that proved to be helpful on this survival journey.

A significant proportion of us modern humans, is still at this level of consciousness. We believe that the universe is a materialistic bunch of random occurrences that do not follow any fixed laws or patterns in their unfolding. In such an imagined universe, in which everything is colliding into everything else we worship the forces of good luck and bad luck. When the things that collide with us help us, we call them good luck, a break, a windfall. When the things that collide with us hurt us, we call them bad luck. To unlock the secret of life that is found within us, we must understand and transcend this primitive level of consciousness called *chance*.

Subconscious conditioning through <u>Superstition</u>

Beyond the emotion of fear and the belief in chance, man evolved to a level of consciousness called superstition. When he observed powerful phenomena like lightening, thunder, rain, floods, volcanos, changing seasons, and the growth and ripening of crops, he concluded that there must be in the outside world a certain power that was making these things happen. This power must be a frightful power because he could not see and touch it. There was evidence of this power everywhere around him meaning that this power was working on the earth, but this power must be enthroned up in the sky, for it was from the sky that the sun, rain, and thunder were all coming, as the most visible manifestations of this power.

Fear became even greater because now, man had become conscious of a mighty power outside of himself. He had more than the wild animals and natural phenomena to run away from. There was an invisible power looking down on him from high above in the sky. He did not know the nature of this power or its intention toward him. Sometimes he was lucky because this power smiled down on him with sun and fruits and a good hunt. Sometimes he was unlucky because this power frowned at him with drought or snow or thunders and volcanoes. The emotion of fear and the belief in chance became translated into superstition, the attribution of the causal forces of the universe to some unpredictable mighty power in the sky.

Subconscious conditioning through <u>Trial and Error</u>

Man used to use stones to hunt down animals for food. We can imagine that on a certain hot sunny dry afternoon he flung a stone toward an animal and missed, but this stone struck a rock and he saw a spark which caught the nearby grass and became a wild fire. We imagine that he ran away from this fire as far as he could and after the fire had run out, he walked through the razed plains in amazement. Then he came upon some roasted cassava and tasted them, and they tasted good. Then he came upon a roasted animal and tasted it, and it tasted better still. And so came the first invention of man; fire, and its application in cooking. As fearful, superstitious man wandered the earth interacting with his environment with the sole purpose of surviving, he relied on chance for the things that happened to him. The things that proved helpful he learned to remember and reproduce. The things that proved hurtful or simply not helpful he learned to avoid. And so, through trial and error, man evolved.

Even with our overrated college degrees, fine clothes and smart technological gadgets, we fail to realize that much of our life is still being lived at this level of consciousness. Life has become like a supermarket in which we try on things like shoes to see if they will fit. Our normal tendency is to give that job a try, give that relationship a try, give that business idea a try, give that treatment a try. And when we try, we expect failure more than we expect success, because hidden in some deep dungeons of our sub-consciousness is this belief that we are living in an unfriendly universe. The major reason why we fail in the things we do is because we were *just trying*, to begin with. Our actions are usually not backed by the commitment to succeed, because our minds are usually devoid of the conviction that we are going to succeed.

By understanding and transcending the trial and error mentality, we will be moving closer to unveiling the secret that lies within up in us.

Subconscious conditioning through Religion

After man had accumulated enough patterns of causation through trial and error, he created the dichotomy of *good* versus *bad* based on how his experiences felt or helped him. Since he was already aware of the presence of invisible forces as the ultimate causes of the visible phenomena of his environment, he also used the process of logical reasoning to arrive at the conclusion that for the good phenomena there were good causal forces or gods, and for the bad phenomena there were wicked causal forces or gods. He noticed to his dismay that he could not respond to the fear instinct by fighting or running away from these gods, since they seemed to be more powerful than him, and he could sense their presence everywhere he went.

He thus evolved a system of living with these gods. The good gods were to be loved and rewarded for their kindness, and the wicked gods were to be feared and appeased. It was a matter of common sense to attribute every major event to a god, or a cause. Thus, man created the god of the harvest, the god of light, the god of fire, the god of fertility, the god of the hunt, etc. In an attempt to find ways of communicating with these gods, man evolved statues and rituals, which with the evolution of language and organized societies, culminated in creeds and systems of worship.

Monotheism is the highest evolution of religion thus far, in which the many gods of the ancient traditions culminate in the Almighty God of Judaism, Christianity, and Islam, the many gods of the ancients now having been translated into the attributes or names of the One God. When you worship "Jehovah my Provider" for example, you are undergoing the same psychological dynamics that our forefathers experienced when they offered sacrifices to the "god of the harvest". It is interesting to note also that while we have created the idea of the Almighty Good God, we have also imported the idea of the evil gods by creating a Mighty Devil or Satan, as the opposite of God.

Thus, the duality-consciousness that was created by superstitious early man, persists in modern religion, and most creeds, dogmas, and systems of worship are based on the fear that if we do not do what God wants, he will hand us over to the Devil for punishment. Doesn't that sound too familiar an analogy for our local judge and jailor? My goal is not to discredit religion but to help you understand it as a conscious process so that you can transcend it and find the deeper truth of your being. Religion is but a curtain behind which hides the Secret Place you are seeking.

Subconscious conditioning through <u>Science</u>

For thousands of years, man evolved as a religious being. Religious traditions were organized and perfected, and the religious masters and prophets became the leaders or messengers of human communities. The wisdom of the enlightened or chosen ones guided societies to create moral codes and systems of living. Heaven was defined as the destiny of humanity. Yes, if the Almighty, All-Good God was in heaven, then what made sense was that when we die we will go and meet him for our reward. And the opposite was true of those who merited punishment.

They must go and meet the Devil whose own address must be the opposite of a heaven up there, that is, a hell down there. Man had finally formulated a meaning for his existence and a framework within which he could create belief systems and moral codes to govern his life. So, religion was the first step to the systematization of human life. The only problem is that it was simply a glorified form of superstition, because it was based on speculation and dogma, rather than evidence. Philosophy emerged out of religion as a tool to take it out of the darkness of superstition to the light of reason.

As recently as 300 years ago, man reached a breakthrough in his evolution. Man merged the data he had accumulated through trial and error, with the philosophical approach, to create a systematic, measurable, verifiable, and reproducible system of interpreting the universe. The excitement was so great. Man was thrilled to finally be liberated from the clutches of the uncertainty of religion. He could actually know the universe through measurements and calculations. And by knowing the universe in this way, he could unveil the laws governing it, and apply these laws to create things. This was the birth of modern science.

Man had become an inventor. Religion was right about one thing, that man was the image and likeness of God. So, when man discovered his creativity, he knew he had found God. The rift between religion and science was formed quite easily and fast. A new dichotomy was formed. We now had the *idealists* (the religionists and philosophers) who believed in the reality of the unseen as the cause of the seen, versus the *realists or materialists* (the scientists) who believed that if it cannot be observed or measured with the tools of science, then it does not exist. The ridicule of the realist or materialist scientist is contained within his own very existence.

The scientist is yet to build an instrument to measure the capacity within himself with which he measures other things. Does that mean that that capacity does not exist? Unfortunately, all the applied sciences such as medicine, engineering and technology, sociology, psychology, economics, politics, etc., are founded on the flawed premise of materialism. Each faction has its own pope: Peter for the Church and Newton for Science. By understanding how this duality evolved, you immediately perceive that there must be something in the space in between.

Subconscious conditioning through <u>Secret societies</u>

From the Dark Ages through the Middle Ages, it is the Church that ruled the western world. The Pope who was the successor of Saint Peter was enthroned as the Vicar of Christ. He ordained bishops, appointed cardinals, and anointed kings. The crowning of kings by the pope endowed them with divine rights. The theories of the early scientists were burned if they contradicted the teachings of the church. Their inventions were destroyed if they had no use or value for the pope. The scientists who had theories and inventions that were useful to the pope were invited to serve the church. Those whose theories and inventions were antagonistic to the teachings of the church were forced to retract their views or be burned alive at the stake, the fate of all who were found guilty of blasphemy in those days.

The earliest fathers of science, the genius thinkers and inventors of old were also devout church folk because at the time the church had the monopoly of scholarship. The ages were Dark, not because the sun was not shining, but because humanity was covered with the blanket of illiteracy and ignorance. So, what would you do if you were among that class of enlightened folks who believed in God and also in science and had proof that God works through science, and your conviction was so strong that you would rather be excommunicated by the pope than retract them? What would you do if you faced excommunication and death, but you really wanted to stay alive and pass your teachings on to the world so that more people could benefit from them? You would do what rat moles do – dig a hole underground.

Secret societies evolved as clusters of 'enlightened' beings who had elaborated scientific methods and teachings that were not accepted by the church. Due to their separation from the church, they sometimes went to certain extremes of teachings that the church found embarrassing, and practices that were branded as pagan. As they took in more and more students and developed their systems into powerful forces of change, they could no longer be ignored. The church needed to take a stand. So, thanks to this 'band of rebels' the human language was blessed with a new term in her vocabulary, *secret societies*.

They were banished from the church and Christians were forbidden from becoming members in such groups. Whether it is a brotherhood or sisterhood, it doesn't matter by what name it is called or which famous inventor, billionaire, or president is or has been a member. Clubs, societies, fraternities, and cults have emerged from this same root of secret societies. They are 'societies' in the sense that they are human communities or masterminds with a defined worldview, organized teaching, and systematic approach to addressing the problems of life. They are 'secret' in the sense that membership is exclusive, members are sworn to secrecy, and membership is incumbent on the completion of certain initiation rites.

The real secret behind secret societies is the fact that their elaborate initiation rites and practice rituals hypnotize the initiate into the belief that it is the power in that society that is giving him the results he is experiencing in his life. These rites and rituals help unlock the power of your sub-conscious mind; the mastermind alliance created by the brotherhood or sisterhood constitutes an enormous reservoir of power you are constantly tapping from to create miraculous results in your life and business; and the oath of secrecy creates the feeling of mystery that serves as permanent food for this hypnotism. But that's about all there is. There is no magic. It is your power that you are using to plug into the pool of collective power created by the collective consciousness of the fraternity.

Unfortunately, the growth of such powerful organizations has also provided a perfect cover for devilish power mongers who have found in them an easy path to nourish their greed. That is why in some cults today the final initiation rites involve sacrificing the life of a family member, or the performance of some task that is invariably destructive to other people or key pillars of human society. It is therefore understandable that at least in theory, the Church views the secret societies as the temples of Satan.

In this book, we will not concern ourselves with the details of how secret societies work. My intention is to help you draw a mind map of how human conditioning has evolved, so that you will get to see even secret societies as a system that has evolved through man's psychological adaptation to his environment. It is a liberating experience to find out that even secret societies do not hold the secret to your freedom. Society has gotten so hypnotized that when someone becomes a president, outstanding scientist, inventor, billionaire, or superstar we must run around to find which secret society he belongs to. It appears they are not that 'secret' these days. Now you know how they evolved and what the essential ingredient of their seeming magic is. You are now free to forget about them and move on.

Subconscious conditioning through <u>Economics</u>

The definition of economics as "the social science that studies human behavior in relation to ends and scarce means which have alternative uses and are governed by the forces of demand and supply" is by far one of the greatest curses that ever befell humankind. The Newtonian materialistic or realistic view of the universe logically gave birth to the paradigm of scarcity, which in turn became the foundation of the field of economics as the mechanism by which men could ration the distribution of these scarce resources. The first implication of a collective belief in scarcity is the fear of lack. When the fear of lack sets in, the survival instinct responds by developing in the individual a new muscle called selfishness.

Man now lives for the purpose of having his needs met, and saving up for the rainy day. Then as possession becomes the only guarantee of security, greed sets in. It is no longer enough to have your needs met. It is no longer enough to have a little bread saved up for tomorrow. Now, we need fancy clothes cars, houses, and fat bank accounts to inflate our egos and show off that we are more successful than the other person, and by implication, more important in society.

Then, the idea sets in that I can't have all that I need to satisfy my vanity, simply by working hard and competing. Thus sets in the idea of using others. When we use other people physically we call it slavery. When we use other people psychologically we call it corruption. By the time we realize it greed, a base emotion that belongs to the lowest of animals, has become so fashionable that we have dressed it in scholastic language and built an altar called Wall Street to worship it. It didn't take long for man to realize that he could raise the demand of a necessity by creating an artificial scarcity. And if he had the power over supply, and the demand was inescapable then he automatically had the power of pricing.

With the invention of currency (money) and the industrial revolution, economics rapidly became a tool in the hands of power mongers. Our current economic systems are based on competition. It would have been a fair game if all were playing on a level field following the same rules. But it is not so. You need not look too deep to notice that the financial institutions and so-called humanitarian organizations in the world are well crafted mechanisms that ensure that there are a few nations (and a few groups of people in these few nations) who are pulling the strings and milking the endowed nations of their resources, while giving them just enough hay to stay alive and keep producing the milk. Where this silent manipulation does not work effectively, or when the giants have a conflict of interest on a certain trophy, they take it by force. That is what war is all about.

In the industrialized countries, the model is replicated. About 99% of the people wake up with their hearts racing in response to adrenaline, eat breakfast on the train, return home completely exhausted with just enough hours to crash and wake up the next day to continue the rat race day after day till they die, while their homes and even the dollar notes that pass through their hands actually belong to a few 1% or even less. Has it ever occurred to you that the dollar bill in your wallet does not belong to you? It is a legal tender, a medium of exchange through which you can get the soda you want while the other person uses it to get the sandwich he wants. On top of the value of what the dollar bill can purchase for you, you are actually paying rent to the invisible owner of that dollar bill.

I want to help you debunk the dogma that we are living in a universe that has scarce resources. A simple Google search will show you that as of the year 2017 there are 2,043 billionaires in the world, with a cumulative fortune of 7.67 trillion US dollars. These billionaires represent 0.00002724% of the world's population. If you distribute their wealth amongst the 7.5 billion people of the world, each person will go away with a little over a thousand dollars. If you distribute their wealth amongst the 327 million Americans, each person will go home with a little over 23,000 US dollars.

If you distribute the collective wealth of these 2,043 people among the 23 million people in Cameroon, the country I come from, each person will go home with 333.5 million dollars, which in the local currency will amount to 167 billion francs. What's my point? If a bunch of fellows small enough to fill my local church at Queen of Peace Parish Njimafor Mbatu, have enough money to make each Cameroonian so wealthy that the wealth can trickle down to their tenth generation and beyond; if these few fellows have so much money that even in mighty America they can turn all citizens into white collar workers and pay them for six months in a row, then you will agree with me that the problem of resources in this world is not that of scarcity, but that of distribution.

I have limited myself to individual billionaires. Imagine what the picture will look like if we bring the millionaires, the corporations, the governments and the churches into the equation. Your poverty is a socially constructed trance in which you have been programmed to passively dance along, wasting your life force to feed the predators that are beating the drum. When you understand how poverty is artificially constructed, you will awaken from this trance, and when you awaken from the trance, you will pop out of the crowd like a bubble.

So, we see that our inherited instincts and social conditioning have created a false sense of security in which we hide like chicks in a nest. The concept of comfort zones is the expression of our propensity for psychological inertia. That which we are familiar with, we tend to cling to. That which we are unfamiliar with, we tend to avoid or run away from. Our default tendency is to swallow whole sale whatsoever our religion, science, social institutions, and all that we consider authority have fed us with. We use these popular standards of normalcy as the molds with which we shape our lives until when tragedy or some life altering experience jolts us and causes us to start thinking.

CHAPTER 5

Transcending Conventional Thinking

The fifth insight

In the preservation room of social conditioning, our thinking capacities are embalmed so that instead of using our brains to think, we use them to conform. Studying means wiring our brains after the pattern that has been laid down by the curriculum. Being religious means wiring our brains after the pattern that has been laid down by the creed, dogmas, and scriptures. Being a political activist means wiring our brains after the pattern that has been laid down by the agenda of the party. Modern man does not think, yet thinking is the one capacity that makes men gods.

Frustrated that neither the FBI nor the National Archives are taking them serious and knowing full well that Ian would steal the Declaration of Independence if they do nothing to prevent him, Ben decides to take the ultimate risk. The only way to prevent the Declaration of Independence from falling into the wrong hands is to steal it himself.

Ben: *[staring at the declaration of Independence mounted in its glass casing inside the National Archives] A hundred and eighty years of searching, and I'm three feet away. Of all the ideas that became the United States, there's a line here that's at the heart of all the others: "But when a long Train of Abuses and Usurpations, pursuing invariably the same Object, evinces a Design to reduce them under absolute Despotism, it is their Right, it is their Duty, to throw off such Government, and to provide new Guards for their future Security." People don't talk that way anymore.*
Riley: *Beautiful, huh? No idea what you just said.*
Ben: *It means, if there's something wrong, those who have the ability to take action have the responsibility to take action. I'm gonna steal it.*

Riley has used his computer analytical mind to do an excellent job of showing Ben how impossible it is to steal the Declaration of Independence. Not even Ian with his armed gang stand a chance. What more of Ben who is alone and unequipped? But Ben thinks differently; the possibility is often within the impossibility.

Ben: *You know, Thomas Edison tried and failed nearly 2,000 times to develop the carbonized cotton-thread filament for the incandescent light bulb.*
Riley: *Edison?*
Ben: *And when asked about it, he said "I didn't fail; I found out 2,000 ways how not to make a light bulb," but he only needed one way to make it work. [sets down a book in front of Riley] The Preservation Room. Enjoy. Go ahead. Do you know what the preservation room is for?*

Riley: *Delicious jams and jellies?*
Ben: *No, that's where they clean, repair, and maintain all the documents and their storage housings when they are not on display or in the vault. Now, when the case needs work, they take it out of the vault and directly across the hall and into the Preservation Room. The best time for us or Ian to steal it would be during the gala this weekend, when the guards are distracted by the VIPs upstairs; but we'll make our way to the Preservation Room, where there is much less security.*

The Riley's of the world consider it their duty to wake us from our dreams and remind us of the facts of life. They believe that the traditions cannot be broken. They try to convince us that we are here to follow the patterns that have been set for us by our ancestors. They are genuinely convinced that only the world's institutions and its established orthodoxy has the power to determine what is good and true, and that any attempt to think beyond their dictates or live beyond their norms is both futile and sinful.

Ben is the prophet who knows that the strength of any monument is also its weakness. The very evidence why something cannot be done, usually carries within it a pointer to how the thing can be done, but of course no one sees it because everyone is locked up in the belief that it cannot be done. When we have been illuminated by the revelation that all fact is mere conditioning that can be changed if we view life from a different angle, we become obsessed with the calling to conquer conditioning and create our own reality.

The prophets and heroes are not those who followed the way they met, but those who made their own way. As Ralph Waldo Emerson succinctly put it, they do not go where the path leads. Rather they go where there is no path and leave a trail. We will now look at the more modern mechanisms by which we are being conditioned on a daily basis, and then conclude with a hint on how to transcend social conditioning and enter the dimension of personal transformation.

Subconscious conditioning through <u>Politics</u>

Politics, as we know it today, has crept into our consciousness quite recently. Ancient man lived in tribes and clans where leaders were chosen from among the fittest and bravest. The leader was the one most capable of leading and protecting the people from enemy tribes. As societies grew bigger, kings became the leaders of the greater nations that embodied many tribes. Throughout history, we see patrilineal monarchies such as among the Egyptians, the people of Israel, and the Medieval Kings of Europe. Although African countries are governed by so-called democratic structures, the people at the grass roots are still clustered under tribal kings. The Kings had absolute authority because the people regarded them as the incarnation of the gods. The feudal lords or 'haves' in medieval times enjoyed their status as the ones the heavens had chosen to bless, while the rest of the people (the 'Serfs' or 'have-nots') gladly served them, in the belief that they were fulfilling God's will.

Even though democratic systems are founded on the ideal of 'government of the people, by the people, and for the people' the reality is often too far removed from the ideal. Our governments are just decorated versions of the ancient kings and medieval lords. The individual presidents may be good men, but the government as an institution usually is not. The mindset we inherited from our ancestors is that of reliance on the state to take care of us. But unfortunately for us, modern politics is as different from ancient tribal leadership as night is from day. There was once a time when government ensured that every citizen had food, shelter, health, education, and a favorable environment to thrive.

Today you are not certain to have a job, and even if you work round the clock, pension is no longer a guarantee. Our modern politicians have no qualms ripping people off their social benefits such as health insurance and safety, in favor of legislations that favor the big corporations and syndicates that secretly sponsor their political careers. In developing countries, in particular, an alarming proportion of people die within ten years of retirement.

We grew up to be used to the adage that "politics is a dirty game". This mindset is so prevalent in many parts of the world, such that the brightest people go on to focus on art, science, engineering, and all the fashionable professions, while mostly the average people end up having time for politics. Why then should we complain when our countries are collapsing under their rule? They usually don't have the brains and hearts required for the roles they occupy, but since the qualified have refused to answer the call, those that are available had better filled the vacancy.

Wake up from the mindset of entitlement. The government owes you nothing, and even if did (constitutionally), I doubt if they are willing to pay their debts. The governments of developed nations are too busy exploiting the endowed nations and making deals with each other to protect the interests of those who put them in power, while the governments of these endowed but less developed nations are too busy changing the constitutions in order to stay in power and continue serving their colonial masters. A good number of them in Africa are now in a race to create a record of the first president to rule for forty consecutive years. And they are not ashamed to call themselves democratically elected leaders. Your good is not their concern. So, my friend, wake up!

Subconscious conditioning through Education

Education used to be based on the holistic premise that each person finds identity, meaning, and purpose in life through connections to the community, to the natural world, and to spiritual values such as compassion and peace. Schools and universities were built with this ambition in mind, and nations and communities used to be proud of their educated men and women. Today, education is a tool through which the modern world commits the atrocity of mass conditioning. The curricula are designed to teach people the essential skills they need to become efficient robots who can turn the economic wheel to keep maximizing profit. The definition of intelligence has been limited to standardized test scores, and one's value in society is now measured by the number of certificates he has accumulated and the prestige of the schools he has attended.

Because of the over-structuring of the school system, children grow up with minds that are used to being controlled and by the time they are adults they have lost every trace of the holy gift of curiosity that children have. We are so engrossed in getting that MBA and rising up the corporate ladder that we scarcely know anything else. In this 21st century there are kids in America who think that Africans live on trees, and I won't be surprised to meet a rocket scientist who has never seen a live chicken. What we call education today is a social opium that has held souls captive, turning the majority of people into pawns inside a computer game. You don't own yourself if you don't control the knowledge you acquire, process, and apply. Schooling does not make you intelligent. Good schooling only makes you a good tool or weapon.

The over reliance on organized education is one of the causes of the decay of society. You will be embarrassed at how ignorant the average physics professor is if you put him in the real world. Even the smartest and bravest of our men and women are proving on a progressive and consistent basis that we are grossly incompetent in solving the problems we have created, talk less of moving society forward. Wall Street is no longer a safe place to invest your money despite its being the temple for our smartest economists and bankers. Our presidential palaces are no longer occupied by men and women who know where the nation is going, despite the fact that we considered them the best among the best through the democratic process.

Conflicts are multiplying around the world and hunger, disease, natural disasters, global warming, and all the grand global challenges are bringing us to our knees while the United Nations, World Bank, and their sister organizations keep us busy with rhetoric and deco. There is not enough intelligence in the classrooms to solve the problems humanity is facing today.

Subconscious conditioning through Media

When I was growing up, my father had a radio set that he operated using batteries. Batteries were expensive, so they needed to be economized. He knew exactly at what time to turn on the radio, and dial a particular channel depending on what he wanted to listen to. We used to have national news, local announcements, then BBC or VOA news. Later on, we had electricity, and we could now leave the radio on all day. Since the channels were few, I knew practically all the names of all the journalists and entertainers and when exactly they came on air. With the information age, things are different. We are now being inundated with information in every form imaginable: radio, satellite television, the internet, books, magazines, bill boards, posters, phones, smartphones, T-shirts, stickers.

More than 99% of the information we are bombarded with on a daily basis is what we did not ask for. If we understand the power of suggestion in shaping the human mind and the effect of the mass suggestion we are subjected to through the countless media outlets, we will realize that physical and even sexual assault pale in comparison to the persistent organized assault on our souls.

Disguised as entertainment, the media conditions our children to become murderers, drug addicts, and sexual perverts. Disguised as publicity, the media conditions us to get sick and depressed so as to become dependent on drugs and all the other gadgets they manufacture. As we collectively contribute to the content of this mass hypnosis, we collectively sedate ourselves into accepting as normal, things that our parents and grandparents would have considered abominable just a generation ago, and that are slowly but surely driving us into a mass grave of our own making.

Subconscious conditioning through the <u>Hard Work Paradigm</u>

I always crack this joke that if hard work was the secret of success, my mother would have been a billionaire and all her children would have been millionaires. Imagine a village woman who brought ten children into the world and had to feed, clothe, educate and shelter them without help from her husband. In my country Cameroon we don't have social security numbers and government benefits. My mother had no formal education and no job. By the time I was born my dad had already attained the official retirement age. He was never a government worker, so there was no pension to fall back on. Imagine the life of my mother; She would wake up every morning at 4:00 am to prepare something for the children to eat and go to school. After we had left for school she would cook a pot of porridge and dish it out into everyone's plate so that we would have something to eat when we returned from school. Then she would set out on rough rocky paths on hills and across valleys for several miles to get to the farm.

Depending on the season, she would till the soil and plant in one farm, then move to another one and harvest something else to bring home in the evening. When she got home in the evening she would again put another giant pot on the fire to prepare supper which we would usually eat around 9:00 pm. On Fridays the older children would meet her at the farm after school so as to carry enough vegetable, grains, or tubers that would be sold in the market on Saturday mornings to get some money with which to buy salt and oil. Fish and meat were a luxury reserved for Christmas or when there was a visitor from the coast.

We the children unconsciously knew that there was no point failing a class exam because it was already hard enough to pay fees for one year, not to talk of affording fees for you to repeat a class. Our immune systems were intelligent enough to know that falling sick meant going to the hospital where they would require money which we did not have. So, we were as healthy as bulls for the most part. As soon as my older siblings got older, they learned how to pull sand out of the nearby streams and sell. There was an abundance of firewood, mangoes, and bitter-leaf on our grandmother's farms in the village mountains some ten miles from where we lived.

It became second nature to us that on some weekends, and during entire vacations we would do this mountaineering to harvest wood, fruits, and vegetables depending on which one was abundant during that season, carry it on our heads and walk another twelve miles to the market, to make a sale. If you carried a load that fetched the equivalent of half a dollar, you were regarded as a giant among your peers. During planting seasons when farm labor was in high demand, we would finish tilling our own farms, then take contracts to till other peoples' farms for money. The equivalent of four dollars for a day's labor for my mother and her three or four able bodied kids was still regarded as a good deal for the family.

This is a tip of the iceberg of the tragedy of trading muscle energy for a loaf of bread to help man survive. You surely have your own story. Even if you grew up under better conditions, I doubt if you are free from the paradigm of hard work as the secret of success. If hard work was what you needed to succeed, how comes there are people who work a hundred hours a week and they still cannot keep up with bills and debts?

How disheartening does it feel to grow up excited about living the American Dream only to be faced with the reality that after having completed university and secured for yourself the esteemed title of doctor, lawyer, pharmacist, accountant, or engineer, you now have to spend the rest of your life working to pay off the college loan, mortgage, taxes, insurance, and credit card debt; and while doing so you barely have time for your family, church, community, and cannot travel and see the world?

We all feel this pain, and my intention is not to add salt to injury, but rather to awaken you from the trance of spinning the wheel like a caged mouse.

While we must apply physical effort in the practical world so that our good can come to us through the regular channels of production, demand, and supply, it is clear to you and I that the secret to life is found beyond the realms of hard work.

Subconscious conditioning through Positive Thinking Paradigm

The early years of the 20th century saw the birth of a new doctrine of "mind over matter". Physicists came up with Quantum Theory to explain their discovery that the world was not just a bunch of atoms, but that the atoms were clusters of subatomic particles, which themselves were made up of even smaller particles. It was discovered that these smallest observable particles called photons had strange properties like being able to be in many places at the same time, responding to the thoughts of the observer, etc.

While the die-hard realists like Einstein died with their conviction that there was nothing in the space between and beyond the sub-atomic particles, another faction quickly concluded that that space must be the field of consciousness of which we are a part. A scientific theory emerged to explain the dogma of belief. This New Thought movement became packaged as The Power of Positive Thinking, Mind Control, Mental Science, Mental Alchemy, Religious Science, and a dozen other names, and began to dominate the popular thought culture as the method through which people could control their lives, influence other people, and create miracles in their businesses and environments.

The premise of new thought is the same as for all the other thought systems before it. It assumes a dualistic reality in which a separated self needs to apply mental techniques to influence an external universe that is otherwise hostile toward him.

Subconscious conditioning through Law of Attraction Paradigm

The unique thing about 'the Law of Attraction' teachings is that it makes an effort to explain using scientific language the mechanism by which things happen to us. By understanding how the universe works, people naturally unfold their faculty of faith, and increase their confidence and ability to apply this law over and over again to answer the questions in their lives, fill their needs, and achieve their aspirations. Thus the 'Law of Attraction' teachings do not present a new discovery, but rather explain in a clearer, more scientific and unreligious way, why we get what we get, and how we can stop getting what we don't want and start getting what we want, deliberately.

If the Law of Attraction is simply the scientific theory explaining the phenomena of 'mind over matter', then it falls within the same domain of 'mind over matter'; that is, it assumes a dualistic reality in which a separated self needs to apply mental techniques to align itself with the laws of an external universe so as to get what it wants. But you will find that the Law of Attraction teaching, beautiful as it sounds, and despite the numerous stories people have reported about its workings in their lives, is not the life gem in itself, but the nut that holds the life gem.

Subconscious conditioning through the Personal Achievement Paradigm

What would you do with your life if you woke up one morning and found that you had a billion dollars in the bank, were enjoying a blissful romance with the partner of your dreams, lived in a magnificent home, had not just the car of your dreams but a private jet as well? What would your life look like if every personal goal were achieved? Most people who get to a place where all the goals they set for themselves have been achieved, go through a crisis. They suddenly feel empty or bored. Some resort to drugs and destructive behavior while others simply commit suicide. A few have found in those crises moments their spiritual awakening in which a new self is born, and they have lived the remainder of their days joyfully giving away the same fortune they had labored so hard to accumulate, but this time around experiencing a fullness and a bliss that the material wealth could not afford.

It is not an accident of evolution that man is a social animal. While you are an individual that is conscious of being a separate entity, your individual self can only be perceived and experienced in the light of the

Universal Individuality or Collective Self. Our beings are constantly flowing into and through one another as the waves on the ocean. The wave you see in this moment does not exist in the next moment, and then in another moment, it reappears as a different wave on a different shore.

If you were a molecule of water within the wave, you would realize that the reality of your existence is the ocean and not the wave. The interconnectedness that is so visible in nature is an indication that we as conscious beings have an even deeper degree of interconnectedness. In fact, it is safe to say that there is only one of us in this world. There is only one being, manifesting and experiencing Itself as the multiplicity of masks or personalities called Zuma, Vidhi, Steve, Obi, Chi, Sabrina, and so on.

Love is therefore not a religious commandment that we are forced to obey or else, go to hell. Compassion and charity are not religious ordinances that we are forced to observe as the currency for blessings. Goodwill and service are not moral codes that we must live by or get thrown in jail. The soul in you has a natural affinity for the soul in the other person because it recognizes it as itself. When you are aware of this Oneness you are in the state of love.

When you open yourself to love through the channels of compassion, service, forgiveness, and goodwill, you feel a natural expansion of your being; that thing you call joy, peace, fulfillment, upliftment. Selfishness creates the opposite effect. When you live for self alone, once that self has eaten of the tree of vanity to its full, the natural thing is a hangover. When you come to the end of self, and are not fortunate to receive timely help, you will destroy yourself. Personal achievement therefore is a conditioning that has evolved over time like all other mental states, but in itself, is not the ultimate purpose of life.

Subconscious conditioning through the <u>Peak Performance Paradigm</u>

Every business exists for profit. A few have added to the profit motive the quest for social impact. 'Corporate social responsibility' has become a cliché that businesses use to make the world see them as being socially accountable or working for the good of people, while the covert motive usually is that a good social image wins more trust and hence more customers, and ultimately more dollars in profit. When companies spend money on continuing professional development and business retreats for their staff, we are often misled into thinking that they are doing charity.

The truth is that the peak performance of their staff is the variable they need to invest in, in order to ensure the peak performance of their companies or organizations in terms of profit, or the achievement of whatever agenda for which the organization exists. Just as it is the natural calling of every person to achieve the greatest level of fruitfulness attainable within the circumstances in which he finds himself, it is also the natural calling for any business to attain the maximum level of productivity through which it can serve its purpose in the environment in which it exists.

There is therefore nothing wrong with Peak Performance as a concept in itself, but everything wrong with the paradigm from which it is approached and the ends toward which it is applied. The fact that the increasing performance, productivity, and technology, is matched with a corresponding increase in global hunger, disasters, diseases, and inequality, is proof that the governments, businesses, and international organizations need a shift in consciousness as well. The paradigm from which we create solutions is wrong, reason why the 'solutions' rather help us create more problems. We as a society need to transcend this social conditioning called peak performance and find that eternal principle by which people and organizations can thrive as individuals while contributing to the thriving of the whole.

The awakening of human consciousness: Transformation

Your life experiences are not the result of what you are consciously thinking, feeling, saying, and doing in this moment. Your life experiences are the spontaneous expressions of the beliefs or convictions that have been programmed or conditioned in your sub-conscious mind. We have found through our inquiry that these beliefs are not the real you, hence they have no power in themselves. You are the power behind your beliefs. You create your beliefs from a certain identity you have assumed yourself to be. Part of this identity we have inherited from the human race as a whole, part from our biological ancestry, part from our parentage, part from our schooling, part from our religion, part from our peers, and part from our personal experiences.

That which you define yourself as, determines your spontaneous reactions to the environment. These unconscious spontaneous responses gradually build up into patterns or beliefs in your sub-conscious, which in turn create your life experiences. Self-definition remains an unconscious process until you enter the state of awareness. This exercise is not intended to create some theories of psychology or philosophy, but to show to the ordinary person like you and me in a practical way, how we have defined ourselves by crediting the gods of fear, chance, superstition, trial and error, religion, science, secret societies, economics, politics, education, media, hard work, mind power, law of attraction, personal achievement, and peak performance, with the power of causation in our lives.

Anything that you acknowledge as having the power to determine your life, you have enthroned as your god. So, from the primitive instinct of fear, to the great motivation of peak performance, we now see clearly how man has evolved as a conscious being through ascending degrees of conditioning. By traveling through time and revisiting this journey we come to the realization that these gods we have created and worshipped as the ruling forces in our lives are not the ultimate powers in our existence. They are our creation.

We have had a direct experience of the Infinite Divine Presence living and moving and having His Being in us, through us, and as us, even as we live and move and have our being in Him, from Him, and for Him. Having found the True Self, the Christ in us, we are finally liberated from the false gods, and all the limiting beliefs by which our lives were defined, simply melt away. When the limiting beliefs are replaced by the true beliefs that are inspired from our new place of Christ Awareness, our outer experiences also begin to change automatically. Miracles begin to flow, and our lives begin to glow. This is the Transformative Experience.

If we could borrow the words of Paul the Apostle in Romans 12:2, then we have come to a logical conclusion as to why the only way to be transformed is *through the renewal of your mind*. To renew does not mean to wash, edit, refurbish, or repair. Transformation it is not about merely changing the old; a new self must be born. Self-improvement is not what we need. Self-Transformation is the only way. Having laid a sufficient groundwork, we may now encapsulate the core theme upon which this book is based, as follows:

The Self is a conscious entity whose activity is *thinking*. The thinking process is a reflective exercise in which the thinker is the object, the subject of thinking (the thought) is the image, and the process of thinking is the mirror. Whether you are thinking about the past, the present or the future; whether the stimulus of the thought is an actual experience or an imaginary one; the thing that you are thinking about is always a reflection of yourself the thinker, and the process of thinking (the mirror of consciousness) is your self-definition; that is, that which you are being aware of yourself as being (your experience of Self). The identity of the Self is therefore defined by the Self; the beliefs or subconscious conditionings of the Self are created by the Self, and the life experience of the Self are created by the Self.

Self-determinism therefore is the law governing man's being, and *self-contemplation* is the process by which this law of self-determinism works. The difference between a sage and a petty thief can be traced back to the quality of this inner experience. Where self-contemplation is an active conscious process we talk of a "reflective being". Where self-contemplation is a passive unconscious process, we talk of a "passive being". Active beings are creative masters of their destiny. Passive beings are reactive victims of fate.

Reflective living is the process of awareness or mindfulness, by which we deliberately give conscious attention to our thoughts, feelings, words, actions, and experiences, and examine them with the intention of making meaning out of them. Reflective living is thus the process of being aware of our awareness or thinking about our thinking. It is the very essence of that way of life that is called 'spirituality' and constitutes the path to enlightenment and the awakening of the inner powers in man. It is through reflective living that man becomes aware of the identity he has adopted and from which he is unconsciously weaving the belief patterns that spontaneously create his experience of life. By becoming aware of the self-concept (identity) and the beliefs, he can determine the truth or falsity of them and thereby deliberately accept and reinforce those that serve him and reject and uproot those that do not serve him. The reflective being deliberately creates the experiences he desires. Reflective living is the path of righteousness, the way to the kingdom of heaven, the chants that bring down the walls of Jericho and ushers us into the Promised Land.

Passive living is the opposite of reflective living. The passive mind functions from a self-concept it is not aware of. His experiences are created from subconscious programs or beliefs he is not aware of. He is unaware of the process by which his identity forms his beliefs and by which his beliefs become his experiences. He attributes the power of causality in his life to an external God and external circumstances, both of which are beyond his control. He believes that his lot is to wait for whatever the capricious forces have willed for his life, then react to them. The passive mind runs on autopilot because the person is under the sedative influence of the senses and is living within the hypnotic trance of the busy external world that these senses report to him as real. The passive being passively receives the experiences that have been spontaneously generated by his inner conditioning, and passively reacts to them, thereby reprogramming them into his subconscious. His life is a vicious circle of varieties of experiences that are in reality altered versions of the same thing. This explains why for example, a person who rushes into a new relationship as an escape from a previous abusive relationship wakes up one day to find that the new partner is simply the old one in different clothing.

We have developed a Success Code which you can use to "code" the next phase of your life the way a software engineer codes a software or mobile application. We have undertaken a journey of consciousness through which we have found that the outer experiences with which we normally identify, are not the true Self. We have taken another journey through time and experienced how our inner conditionings have evolved, and by so doing we have uprooted the limiting beliefs that have been controlling our lives. Having died to the old, we are now ready to resurrect as the new.

CHAPTER 6

Purpose, Passion, Persistence

The sixth insight:

In order for the things in your life to change, you must change the things in your life. You must become "white hot" with desire in order to trigger the laws by which your mind begins orchestrating the universe to bring about the good you desire. We spend our lives complaining about our circumstances and hoping that our lives will change the day the things outside of us change – the government, our employer, our partner, the economy, and so on. What we fail to realize is that nothing changes for us unless we change who we are. The universe is always matching our experience with the state we are occupying in consciousness. In order for us to see a change, we must be the change. And the key is in the 3Ps: Passion, Purpose, Persistence.

Disguised as a guest, Ben enters the National Archives during a gala evening. From his computer lab in a van parked outside, Riley directs Ben remotely, and directs him to the location of the Declaration by maneuvering through the security system he had hacked into. He steals Abigail's fingerprints from a switched wine glass and clones them into a key that he uses to break into the preservation room. He succeeds to steal the Declaration of Independence, just in time to be spotted by Ian and his men as they break in through their own underground channel. A gun chase begins downstairs while up in the gala hall, Abigail has become suspicious and it is now clear that Ben's name is not on the guest list.

Ben tries to leave via the gift shop and logically, he must "buy" the Declaration. The clerk does not know that what he is carrying is the real thing that he has stolen from the preservation room. She thinks it is one of the souvenir copies on sale. He pays for two, and walks away.

Abigail has been looking for him everywhere. She knows that something is not right. She catches Ben just as he is walking out the front door. She seizes the Declaration from Ben, only to get kidnapped moments later by Ian's men.

Ben and Riley rescue Abigail in a hot car chase around the streets of D.C. but the Declaration is left behind with Ian. Agent Sadusky and his FBI team are in hot pursuit.

While in the van with Ben and Riley, *Abigail is freaking out, thinking that she has just left the Declaration with Ian.*

Ben: *They don't have it.[Pulls the Declaration out to show her]*
Ben: *See, now can you please stop shouting?*
Abigail: *Give me that!*
Ben: *You're still shouting. And it's really starting to annoy. You would do well, Dr. Chase, to be a bit more civilized in this instance.*
Abigail: *If that's the real Declaration, what did they get?*
Ben: *A souvenir. I thought it might be a good idea to have a duplicate, turns out I was right. Actually, I had to pay for the real one and the duplicate, so you owe me $35, plus tax.*
Riley: *Genius.*

Abigail: *Verdammt! Give me that!*
Ben: *You know something? You're shouting again.*
Riley: *I'm pretty sure she was swearing, too.*
Ben: *Well, I probably deserved that.*

Most people think that the purpose of life is the American Dream – getting just enough education that will enable to secure a job from which you will earn a check to pay for the nice little house and car, raise a cute little family, save up for retirement, and hopefully go for a few vacations. This flawed sense of purpose also creates a disease called "job reliance", that turns people into puppets that go about just doing their job, retiring, getting old, and waiting to get the hell out of here. There is a great distinction between your job and your work. You are doing your authentic work if:

- You are doing something because you love it, not just because it helps you pay the bills.
- You are doing the work you really want to do, not the job that is available.
- You often act spontaneously, creatively.
- You do it with ease and dexterity. You feel like you are a genius at it because it flows naturally from your inner self.
- Every morning you look forward to work with joy, and every evening you come home feeling fulfilled and grateful.
- Your work gives you the opportunity to express your real self. Your originality and uniqueness shines through what you do. You are not just an invisible cock in the corporate wheel.
- In the course of doing your work you have the opportunity to develop your own capacities and grow into a better person.
- You feel energized rather than drained when you are at work. Fresh energy and fresh ideas pour out of you when you are working.
- You enjoy a mutually supportive relationship with the people you work with and feel like a member of a family that shares a common vision.

- When you are immersed in your work, you do not notice time passing.
- Your work allows you time for other things that are important in your life like family, exercise, recreation, and spiritual growth.
- Your work fetches you enough money to pay for the quality of life that you fill fulfilled in.
- Your work gives you the opportunity to be of direct service to as many people as you desire
- Your work is a means for you to fulfill your life purpose. It is clearly a logical step toward achieving your life goals.
- You will still do the work with the same passion, if you had to work for free.
- Above all, your work makes you feel that you are a part of something that is greater than you.

The reason why we are tied to our jobs is because we are in pursuit of money, right? If we had all the money we needed, it would afford us the freedom to start living our true purpose, and consequently, our authentic lives. That is the general thinking, but what if I told you that jobs don't make people rich.

Forty-year old Floyd Mayweather is an American professional boxing promoter and retired professional boxer. He competed from 1996 to 2017, held 15 world titles in five weight classes and the linear championship in four different weight classes (twice at welterweight), and retired with an undefeated record of 49 fights. Twenty-nine-year-old Conor McGregor is an Irish professional mixed martial artist and professional boxer who is currently signed to the Ultimate Fighting Championship (UFC). He is the reigning, UFC Lightweight Champion and former UFC Featherweight Champion. During his mixed martial arts (MMA) career, McGregor has competed as a featherweight, lightweight, and welterweight. As of 2017, McGregor is ranked 3rd on UFC's pound for pound rankings.

When McGregor challenged Mayweather to a fight, and Mayweather accepted to come out of retirement and take the bait, boxing fans knew that they had been gifted with what they called the fight of the century. There was no official boxing title at stake, but the charismatic and entertaining nature of both athletes was enough to make this fight a flood of money. I am not a boxing fan. I just happened to have seen a Mayweather interview on television a few days to the fight. What got me interested was the amount of money he said he would walk away with from that much-awaited fight of August 26ᵗʰ, 2017. I was intrigued to hear a human being call himself a walking ATM, on a Live TV show in America. That got me interested in finding out what this guy knows or does that others don't.

According to media reports, McGregor was guaranteed $US30million and Mayweather guaranteed $US100million for the fight purse alone. Other sources of revenue included the pay-per-view, promotion, sponsorship, drinks, and gate revenue. The purse is the amount that both fighters make, regardless of the financial success of the fight through ticket sales and pay-per-view purchases. Even if zero fans had watched the fight between Mayweather and McGregor on Saturday night, the two already had huge amounts headed their way. The Pay Per View (PPV) figures were predicting to surpass 4.9 million PPVs, netting upwards of $US750million. Selling off premium advertising space on his clothing, Mayweather reportedly made an incredible $31.6 million ($US25m) before even setting foot in the ring against McGregor. Mayweather, being a co-promoter of the fight, is reported to have walked home with a profit of $US350 million, if not more, while McGregor walked home from the highest pay day of his life ever, with $US100 million. Of course, these are all estimated figures, but for the purpose of this book, they don't need to be exact.

I have told you that I am not a boxing fan. My interest in this fight is the money. How and why on earth will two guys throw blows at each other inside a ring for a few minutes, and walk away with a collective revenue of over half a billion dollars? I don't know Mayweather personally but when I saw him on TV he appeared and sounded too simple, humble, composed, and natural, for the kind of money that was being called in association with his name. When the TV presenter asked if people like him go to the ATM, he simply said "I am a moving ATM". When he was teased as to how banks manage customers like him, he candidly told the audience that the banks deliver his money at home in trucks. And when he was asked how much, out of all his money, he could really carry around at one time, he said $US50million. The boxing itself lasted for less than an hour, so if these guys were just doing a job, how much do you think they would have earned per hour? But they are not jobbers. They are wealth creators who have money working for them because they are busy doing something they are passionate about. Money comes to them through advertising, ticket sales, drink sales, pay-per-view, and broadcasting rights.

Depending on which educational system we were raised in, we spend between seventeen and twenty-two years in school so as to graduate with the certificates that will guarantee us the best salaries and a VIP seat at every gathering. The U.S. Bureau of Labor Statistics ranks jobs according to median annual salary, unemployment rate, and number of projected jobs. The current data is shown on the table below:

Rank	Job Title	Median annual salary
1	Anesthesiologist	$187,200.00
2	Obstetrician and Gynecologist	$187,200.00
3	Oral and Maxillofacial Surgeon	$187,200.00
4	Orthodontist	$187,200.00
5	Physician	$187,200.00
6	Psychiatrist	$187,200.00
7	Surgeon	$187,200.00
8	Pediatrician	$170,300.00
9	Nurse Anesthetist	$157,140.00
10	Dentist	$152,700.00
11	IT Manager	$131,600.00
12	Petroleum Engineer	$129,990.00
13	Marketing Manager	$128,750.00
14	Pharmacist	$121,500.00
15	Prosthodontist	$119,740.00
16	Podiatrist	$119,340.00
17	Financial Manager	$117,990.00
18	Lawyer	$115,820.00
19	Sales Manager	$113,860.00
20	Mathematician	$111,110.00
21	Optometrist	$103,900.00
22	Computer Network Architect	$100,240.00

23	Software Developer	$98,260.00
24	Nurse Practitioner	$98,190.00
25	Physician Assistant	$98,180.00
26	Business Operations Manager	$97,730.00
27	Actuary	$97,070.00
28	Psychologist	$94,590.00
29	Medical and Health Services Manager	$94,500.00
30	Nurse Midwife	$92,510.00

Source: https://money.usnews.com/careers/best-jobs/rankings/the-100-best-jobs? sort=median-salary (Accessed, 08/18/2017)

I know that the majority of people reading this book will not find their job among the thirty job titles above and will not boast of annual incomes of $100,000.00 or above. That is exactly the point of this chapter. If you are a top-ranking doctor, you may be going home with $300,000.00 a year. If you are a top ranking corporate executive or the president of the United States, you may be going home with $500,000.00 a year. Now, if the best paid employee earns $500,000.00 in a year, and Mayweather just made $350million in one day (in fact, in slightly under an hour), what we are saying is that Mayweather made in one hour, enough money to pay the annual salaries of over one thousand of the highest earning doctors, or seven hundred top executives, including the president of the United States. The picture gets even more interesting when you put this Mayweather guy on a scale with the billionaires.

We suddenly realize that the guy is not even rich, compared to the really rich. This brings us to my conclusion that there are not enough hours in a day, there are not enough weeks in a month, there are not enough months in a year, and there are not enough years in a lifetime, if your only chance of being financially free, rich, and really wealthy, is through earning a salary from your job. When we ask the wrong question, we wind up with the wrong answer, and our social conditioning causes us always to ask the wrong question so that we will wind up with answers that will perpetuate our dependence on the systems that control us. The American dream is a hoax to keep you in the hypnotic state. Wake up, and you will find that there are a million ways by which you can live a better life.

Each time you ask, "how do I get out of debt and secure enough income to live in freedom and joy?" the answer often is, "make enough money". And when you ask, "how do I make more money?" the most available answer is, "get another degree, change careers or get an extra job, work harder, etc." While a majority of people think along these lines and stay in the money hypnosis, a tiny minority think differently, and live outside the money hypnosis. Some people are so free that money is as natural to them as the air they breathe. They don't sweat about it. What then is it that they know that the majority don't? What is it that they do that the majority don't?

Rich people know that what brings a ceaseless abundance of money is not the hourly wage from the job, but the systems they have built for themselves. There are two paradigms or approaches to making money: the *effort-based approach*, and the *systems-based approach*. The effort-based approach is what has been programmed into the subconscious minds of the majority of the people, and it is this programming that keeps them within the illusion of never-having-enough. You graduate from college with a prestigious degree, pick up the job of your dreams, and you are all set for the American dream, or its equivalent in whichever country you find yourself. But before you know it, the college loan, the mortgage, the taxes, and the credit card debt are breathing down your neck like a frightful predator. Your flight-fight response sets in and your life becomes an adrenaline pump. The more you chase the dollar, the deeper you dig your grave inside the money hypnosis. Meanwhile the few wealthy guys around us know that the freedom they seek is not in the job, but in the systems they have built, to continuously pump money into their lives, while they are busy doing the things they really enjoy.

You are not living your passionate and authentic life because you are not living your true purpose. You are not living your true purpose because you are busy with your job. You are busy with your job because you need the job to raise the dollars you need to pay the bills. You never have enough of the dollars to catch up with the mounting debts, bills, and increasing cost of living, so you give in more energy, more time, more everything to the job so that you can earn more. And by the time you die, if you are among the 20% that are debt free, then you are blessed. If you are among the 80% that are still in debt, then you are just normal.

This vicious circle is what I call the money hypnosis. What most people don't realize is that the money hypnosis is a control system that is based on a lie. You don't need your job, because your job is not where your wealth is flowing from. Jobs are meant to give you enough bread to survive enough as a person, while spinning the wheel that is making someone else rich. For you to be free and live your authentic life, you must be free from the want of money. For you to be free from the want of money, you must be living your purpose, outside the illusion. Knowledge is what gets you outside the illusion. When you see the lie for what it is, you will choose to step out and begin a new life on a different plane, even if everyone around you thinks you are crazy. When Jesus said "you shall know the truth and the truth shall set you free", what he meant was that it is only the light of knowledge that can free you from the senseless vicious circle you call life, and place you in the domain where you will live on purpose, passion, and persistence.

CHAPTER 7

Synchronicity

The seventh insight:

When you pursue your purpose with passion, you eventually get to the place where you are so immersed in your quest that it is as if it is the purpose that now possesses you. At this stage you lose touch with time, fear, doubt, and worry, and your life flows like a river. This is the state called synchronicity. You are in a state of resonance with the universe, such that the universe is now orchestrating itself to work in your favor.

The trio drives to Patrick's house (Ben's father). Patrick is terribly scared to learn that Ben has stolen the Declaration of Independence. Ben has finally promoted himself from an outcast in the academic world to a fugitive. He is screwed, and Patrick has been right all this while. The Gates have been just a family of fools chasing after fools' gold. The treasure is just a fantasy. Look what his son has gotten himself into.

Their combines intelligence enables them to study the Declaration document without destroying its delicate paper. They discover an *Ottendorf cipher* written in invisible ink. The message refers to the *Silence Dogood* letters written by Benjamin Franklin. Patrick formerly owned these letters, but he had recently donated them to the *Franklin Institute*. Patrick, whose interest had been won temporarily at the unmasking of the codes behind the Declaration becomes thoroughly sour again at the discovery that it is not the map to the treasure, but just another clue. Abigail who is supposed to be a captive is now curious. She is captivated by Ben's conviction and the map she has just seen. If Ben was right about an invisible treasure map at the back of the Declaration she has been guarding all this while, what else could he be right about?

The three head for the Franklin Library in Philadelphia to find the Letters. The Letters are in display in the library and it is a busy day with people coming in and going out. They cannot be stolen. Using a school boy to acquire the letters' key words, Ben, Riley, and Abigail decode a message pointing to the bell tower of Independence Hall. There, they find a hidden cache containing a pair of glasses with multiple colored lenses invented by Benjamin Franklin, which, when used to read the back of the Declaration reveal a clue pointing to the symbol of Trinity Church which is located on Wall Street and Broadway in New York City.

Abigail, the keeper of the National Archives, a government employee who is supposed to be trying to stop Ben from tampering with the

Declaration of Independence, is now Ben's team mate. Her curiosity and expertise become an asset to Ben. Riley cannot go into the Franklin Institute in person for fear that he will be spotted. So, he uses a school boy to decode the *Ottendorf cipher* from the *Silence Dogood* letters inside the building. Even Patrick, who had given up on the idea of the treasure has his excitement renewed, though for just a brief moment.

What this portion of the movie portrays is that when you pursue your purpose to the point where the purpose takes over your life, the universe begins to orchestrate itself to work for your good, by bringing to your aid, forces that you did not know existed, or forces that you would never have been able to mobilize on your own. The universe is a living presence. The spontaneous unfolding of the universal laws are beyond space, time, human effort, and all the limitations to which our lives are subjected. When we are driven by a compelling purpose to the level where we practically die to our fears, we tune into the frequency of this spontaneously unfolding universe, such that our life becomes the spontaneous blossoming of the universe. This is the experience of synchronicity, the state in which it is no longer us who are living, but the universe living through us.

It is your duty to become all that you can be. Man is the manifestation of God and is here to glorify or give expression to God. An apple tree has only one logical destiny – to bear apples. Your destiny is to bear fruits that reflect the attributes of the Creative Spirit that you really are. You are here to thrive and not just to survive. You ought to be living like royalty, because indeed you are the heir of God, the prince or princess of heaven and ruler over the earth. We all have an equal chance of making it in life. No two people are created to walk the same path. If you look hard enough, you will realize that we all have opportunities that are suited to our unique circumstances. The number one cause of failure therefore is our tendency to pay attention to someone else's strengths and opportunities rather than our own. In so doing, we fall into the state of disharmony with the universe as fear, doubt, worry, judgement, greed, anger, and envy become our dominant emotions.

How different would your life be if you could remind yourself every day that one day you have to leave this earth, and you know not the time, place and means? What would you want the world to remember you for? Until my mother passed, four years ago, I had always had the impression of her being just an insignificant village housewife. But the sermons, eulogies, and testimonies at her funeral have caused me to redefine my concept of greatness. To be great, to be prosperous, to be successful in life, to be a saint, has nothing to do with the conditions under which you were born, how much education you have received, how socially influential you are, and how much money you have in the bank. Love, faith, humility, sincerity, tolerance, patience, forgiveness, purpose, hard work, compassion, dedication, gratitude, and a smile. These are the qualities of the truly great. Truly great people measure their success by the number of lives they have touched. With all my education, impressive curriculum vitae and elaborate leadership career, I still doubt the fact that if I die today, more people will show up and say nicer things about me than they did for my mother. Yes, I fully intend to get my own fair share of all the good things of this life, but I will never forget the lesson my mother taught me by her life.

We often live out of alignment with our purpose and thus out of alignment with the universe, because we have been conditioned to believe only in what we can see. Did the Master not say that "If only you believe you will see the glory of God"? So why do you turn the law up-side-down and expect things to work for you? Don't wait to see before you believe because you will have to wait forever. It is your believing that brings the reality to visibility. Most people don't know what they want; Others know what they want but have an excuse for not having it; It is only a minority of people that knows what they want and will stop at nothing till they get it. For those who chose to walk by faith, all things have a way of working for their good.

Believe in your ability to receive the good you desire. Believe in the universe's willingness to give you the good you are asking for. If you truly believe in God's absolute goodwill toward you, you will have no problem abandoning yourself to His Will. Believe in yourself and the world will believe in you. What others give to you is what you have first given to yourself. Your outer experience is nothing more than a rebroadcast of the reality you have already lived within.

The bridge between success and failure, wealth and poverty, wisdom and stupidity, joy and sorrow, is in this simple three lettered word, "WHY". Those who have a reason for living possess a sense of purpose, direction, passion, and persistence, and are more likely to brave every storm and go the extra mile to bring their desires into fruition. Those without these qualities are at the mercy of every wind, and then they wonder why their own life is so different. The moment you sit back, look deep into your inner self, and resolve that you are going to give your life a meaning no matter what, you have begun to recreate your life.

Strive to be at peace with yourself at all times. When you are at peace with yourself, that peace rubs off everyone you meet and everything you do, just like the perfume you wear leaves its fragrance everywhere you pass. Make a deliberate choice that your life will be pulled by your inner convictions and aspirations rather than pushed by circumstances. When you find your purpose and align yourself with it, you will know the peace that surpasses understanding. Inner peace is a sign that the universe is sending to you, kind of telling you that "I've got your back".

I don't need to read huge philosophical volumes in order to master the secrets by which my life becomes so in harmony with the universe that the universe starts conspiring for my good. I learned quite a deal from my mother who was a peasant farmer. Here is one of them. When you entrust mother earth with a grain of corn and attend to it diligently, nature will reward you with a thousand grains for a harvest. The key to receiving is *giving*. It has pleased the Father to give you the kingdom. All things are already yours. The art of living is about knowing how to receive and enjoy that which is already yours by divine right. You are as important to God as though you were the only human being He created. That's the meaning of "His Infinite Love".

There is an ideal place where you belong in this universe. In that place you owe no bills, you are not afraid of the landlord, you have no debts, there is no tension in your home due to your inability to provide. In that place, you have work that you enjoy doing, money comes effortlessly and in abundant supply, you are vibrant with good health and happiness, and love, peace and blessings are all you give and receive. This ideal place is your reality, and you enter into it through the art of giving.

If a thing is worth believing in, you will believe in it and stick with it even if the heavens come tumbling down. Your dreams and desires are the precious children you came here to give birth to. Believe in the sacredness of your ideals, for only through originality can you be a blessing to the world. Ask no one for permission to act. Be yourself because the universe knows who you are and is committed to helping you express your authentic self but will not help you if you are busy being something or someone that you are not.

Whenever you come face to face with an opportunity, decide whether you are ALL IN or ALL OUT. Hanging on the fence is the syndrome that has made many of us mediocre, poor, weak and unproductive. When you are ALL IN, there is no room in you for doubt, fear, speculation, and distraction; you don't listen to the nay-sayers, and you don't budge in the face of adversity. A shoe mender who is ALL IN usually becomes more successful than an uncommitted car dealer. When you are at the cross roads of life; when you need to make tough choices, go hungry, take risks, face your fears, sweat it out, and tremble in tears and prayer; more often than not, you are on your own. Those are the times that really matter in a person's life. Commitment will always win for you the favor of the universe and summon to your aid forces you never knew existed.

So, when you are about to take that giant leap, or when the tides start turning in your favor and those friends and relatives come flooding in with their volunteered abundance of advice and criticism, please do the one thing that you must do. Tell them to give you a break. Believing in your dream will open your eyes to the opportunities that have always been there for you. Give your dream your full commitment, and your dream will return the favor.

Everyone lives in a spiritual atmosphere of his own making. Your pattern of thought, feeling, speaking and acting determines the quality of your spiritual atmosphere; and the quality of your spiritual atmosphere in turn determines your life experience. The universe is an infinite ocean of love, abundance and well-being, in which we all live and move and have our being, like the fish in the sea. How on earth can something ever go wrong with you?

The quality of your attention in this moment determines the character of your spiritual atmosphere. Pray today as though this was your last day; forgive today as though this was your last day; love today as though this was your last day; do your work today as though this was your last day; play and laugh today as though this was your last day. Your desires are intelligent energy. They know where they are coming from, they know where they are going, and they know how to get there. You are just a channel for the outpouring of infinite possibilities. Stay in the flow and your part is done.

One of the ways to stay in a sublime spiritual atmosphere is to play the gratitude game. Challenge yourself that in every moment, in every place and in every person, you will find something to be thankful for. If you adopt this way of life, before long, your consciousness will become so saturated with gratitude that there will be no room for complaining, criticizing, worry, doubt and fear. When this happens, you would have unlocked the secret door to the ceaseless flow of blessings. Paying attention to the wonderful things in your life is the easiest way to awaken the flame of gratitude and joy which naturally melts away all that you do not want.

Our primary duty in this world is not that of giving other people the pleasure of becoming what they want us to be. Our primary duty in this world is that of doing justice to the infinite potential that is within us and becoming the best that we can be, each in his own unique way. You didn't come here to conform to the standards and past experiences of your family, work place, tribe, or nation. It is your prerogative to choose the quality of life you want to live, decide the mark you want to leave behind, then go to work and make it happen.

Part of our frustration comes from the fact that we wake up every morning with a long list of what we want to get. Change this habit. Wake up every morning with a list of what you want to give and see the magical effect it will have on your life. Stop thinking that you are better or less than everyone else. You are not, and there is no need chasing such an illusion. Rather, work every day to be better than the person you were yesterday. That's where true power lies. You will have faith in yourself if you remind yourself that you were placed here by a higher power to serve a higher purpose than yourself. You will have the courage to pursue your dreams if you remind yourself that your ideas are not your creation, but the stream of eternity flowing through you.

As much as it is within your means to give, please go ahead and give. Give without judging; Give without discriminating; Give without asking for compensation; Give without waiting to be asked; Give without demanding a balance sheet. Since the beginning of time, the sun has been shining and giving life to the earth and not even once has it ever said, "you owe me". My mother, without status, education, or formal employment, spent 56 years of her life giving unconditionally to her husband, ten children, and her community. Never in my life did my mother ever give me the impression that I owed her something. Giving and sharing were the only things she really knew how to do. Like her mother before her, she gave and shared even while on her sick bed and prayed for us even while taking her last breath.

I do not consider it a coincidence that both my mother and grandmother spent their last moments on this earth with me, and that their dramatic exits were amazingly similar. The greatest wisdom that has shaped my life was not acquired from my university professors but from these two amazing women. Let giving be your joy, and giving to you will be the joy of the universe. When your habitual thoughts, words and actions respond to the felt needs of the people around you, you become a valuable presence in your community.

When you are a valuable presence in your community, success, wealth and goodness flow to you spontaneously. And when you are a truly successful person, one who has sown seeds of love in the hearts of people, only then will you wear that elusive crown called self-fulfillment. One of my privileges as a health professional is that I get to watch people die in the hospital wards, or take part in manipulating their corpses in the mortuary during that frightful event called an autopsy. I can tell you from experience that it is impossible to fake a happy death, and it is impossible to mistake a holy death. There is always something magical that happens in the room in the immediate moments after a holy, happy, and fulfilled soul leaves the body.

Also, just as you leave your body odor on your clothes, the human spirit leaves its signature on the body it leaves behind at the moment of the transition called death. If you are observant you can easily tell the difference between a person who died fulfilled versus the one who died in regret or uncertainty. So, there is no escape. Fulfillment is a blessing reserved only for beings who spent their lives lighting up the hearts of other people with love. You can be president of the United States and be unfulfilled. You can be a billionaire and be unfulfilled. You can be a multiple award-winning movie star or artist and be unfulfilled. Love is the only currency of heaven. It is only when you have love that all these external things have meaning. In the absence of love, material success becomes a curse. Love is the real business of your life. Find avenues through which you will be a gift to the world, and turn that into your work.

Your supply is not your job or your business. Your supply is the infinite sea of substance that is found in God and eternally pressing forward in search of avenues through which to overflow. Your job or business is the means through which you sow into the garden of the universe, and through this sowing open up channels for receiving from Infinite Supply. If you recognize this as true, then your questions will change from, "what can I get?" to "what can I give?"

The person who thinks in terms of getting, lives in stress and worry, and builds his career around the idea of competition, which invariable amounts to cheating or using people to maximize profit. The person who thinks in terms of giving, is always preoccupied with strategies through which he can bring about an increase of life to more and more people. This mindset aligns him with the law of increase that animates the universe, and so he becomes a natural avenue of creativity and expansion.

Your job is to know what you want, create the inner experience of having it now, condense this inner experience from the invisible to the visible realm through a corresponding action, then allow the universe to do its part. Just as the sower knows not how the seed turns into a fruit-bearing tree, you need not bother about how your good will come to you. You don't know how electricity works but you have never said "I will stay in the dark till I understand how this stuff works before I benefit from it". We can say the same of your iPhone, your car, even your heartbeat. The miracle working power of the universe is far beyond your comprehension. Figure out what you can, and the universe will figure out what it must. Infinite Intelligence always orchestrates the universe to clothe you in the manifestation of your inner state, using the fastest, easiest, most harmonious path.

Your awareness of being part of a spontaneously creative universe, is the faith with which you create your own life. You create by deliberately choosing the feelings or beliefs you want to experience about any subject that is of interest to you, and then applying the law of correspondence by condensing that feeling into a corresponding action. The secret of creating your life therefore boils down to "faith working through love". Faith creates the spiritual essence of the thing; love gives flesh to the spiritual essence you have created. When you have played your part as a co-creator with God, the universe will never fail to fulfill its own part of the bargain. Universal Law can never be broken.

The universe is in love with you and desires to help you. When you are living for a purpose that is greater than you and your life is all about giving of yourself to serve, empower, and enrich others, you transcend the domain of the rational mind and ego and make your habitation in the domain of the spirit. You pursue your purpose with passion and persistence, while making love, faith, gratitude, and joy your way of life. Here you enter the state of synchronicity with the universe, and the universe makes it its duty to gather and bring to your aid forces that you never knew existed. Even enemies begin working for your good.

CHAPTER 8

Adversity

The eighth insight:

The reason why we think in terms of success and failure is because we subconsciously assume that life is a straight line. When we do not get what we want, when we want it, how we want it, and where we want it, we say that we have failed. Other times we call ourselves failures because we are comparing ourselves with other people and using their story as the standard for our own life. The truth is that there is no such thing as failure. What appears as failure are only setbacks and detours that the universe places on our path to redirect us to where we should be going. Your gift lies within your story. Your opportunity lies within your adversity. If you embrace your challenges and really contemplate them rather than run away from them, you will find the secret key hidden within them for you.

The group is chased by both the FBI and Ian's associates. Ben is arrested by the FBI, while Abigail and Riley lose the real Declaration to Ian. However, Abigail convinces Ian to help them rescue Ben in exchange for the next clue. Ian agrees. He calls Ben to arrange a meeting:

Ian: Hello, Ben. How are you?
Ben: Um, chained to a desk.
Ian: Sorry to hear that. I want you to meet me on the flight deck of the USS Intrepid. You know where that is?
Ben: New York.
Ian: Meet me there at ten o'clock tomorrow morning. And bring those glasses you found at Independence Hall. Yeah, I know about the glasses. We can take a look at the Declaration, and then you can be on your way.
Ben: And I'm supposed to believe that?
Ian: I told you from the start, I only wanted to borrow it. You can have it. And the glasses. I'll even throw in the pipe from the Charlotte.
Ben: I'll be there.
Ian: And tell the FBI agents listening in on this call if they want the Declaration back, and not just a box of confetti, then you'll come alone.

Of course Ben does not go alone. The FBI has taken every security measure to ensure that Ben and Ian do not get out of sight and sound. But the two criminal minds have factored that into their meeting. Ben escapes from FBI custody.

Life is a dance. Life is fun. Life is effortless. The rivers, the forests, and the fields, they all say 'yes, yes, it is so'. We are here to celebrate life, not to merely struggle through life. When genius is at work, life is fun. So, when you find yourself trying too hard, realize that you are acting from the standpoint of weakness. Usually you are trying so hard because instead of giving your whole heart to the process, you are busy trying to control the outcome. Retreat into your inner chamber, reconnect with your inner genius, then come out and act like a person of power.

What will happen if things don't turn out the way you planned? Will you pick the pieces and move on with life as a better, wiser and stronger person, or will you crash? Will you look back and smile and move on in confidence of a brighter tomorrow, or will you freeze with self-criticism, regret, shame and fear? The way you react when things don't turn out the way you planned, is a strong indicator of *detachment* and detachment is the spiritual quality you cannot do without if you are to live a happy and fulfilled life.

Learn to be detached about life. Don't take things too personal. If you allow success to get to your head, you will sooner or later become too self-confident, boastful, and vain. If you allow failure to get the better of you, you will soon get to the place where you are so frustrated and afraid that you are frozen into inaction. Whatever you are involved in, give it the best of yourself, then detach from the outcome. You can detach from external outcomes only when you are animated from within because you are living from a compelling *why*.

As the saying goes, "tough times never last, but tough people do". Are you going through tough times? Do you have some urgent need to fill? Do you have some challenge to meet? Most of us are. That is why we are always seeking for something more in life. The first thing you should know is that no matter the gravity or nature of your problem, it is only temporary. Life is dynamic, not static. Whatever is happening to you now will pass away as surely as the darkness gives way to the light of the new day.

Tough times happen to all men and women who live on this planet. So, console yourself by knowing that you are not alone, that you are where you are not because life is unjust to you, but because of specific causes which when identified, will turn your life around like a miracle. The storms of life are nature's goodwill gesture to shaken us and wake us from the slumber of mediocrity, into the real life of abundance that we were created to live.

The greatest leaders, inventors and saints that humanity has ever known, were the children of adversity. There is hardly any wealthy man worthy of the name, who was not born poor, and who has not suffered most, if not all the hardships you are currently going through. All the heroes we know today, once reached the point where they nearly gave up, but thank God, they hung on a little longer. It is same for you, hang on a little longer and before you know it, your breakthrough will rush in like a tide. You know, it is at midnight, when the darkness is thickest, that the dawn begins to break in. The greater your trouble, the greater the miracle that awaits you.

If you walked with the assurance that the Supreme Power of the universe is with you, in you, and through you, you will never again experience fear or doubt. To he who has faith, all the forces, circumstances and events in the world are always conspiring to help, rather than hurt him. No matter the seeming turbulence, all things work together for his good. Always remember this. It is not you that is living life; It is Life that is living Itself AS you. Your conscious awareness of the Omnipotent Presence within you, is the possession of all things attainable.

No matter how fierce the fires or storms that confront you in life; no matter how thick and tall the walls that try to stop you from reaching your goals; always bear in mind that the only way to your destination is THROUGH them. There's no doubt that on your life's journey, there will come moments of trial when you feel like the goal is not worth it, that you've been wasting your time, that perhaps your critics were right, that throwing in the towel is the best thing to do. Here's what every hero knows from experience, "when you feel like fainting, that's the moment you shouldn't faint because success waits to embrace your very next step".

Remain cool and unruffled under all circumstances. Stay calm. Do not be overwhelmed by the size of the problem; do not be overcome by fear. Look the problem in the face and you will realize that most of what we call problems are not problems at all. They are simply ghosts, which our fears and worries have created in our imagination, and invested with the power to destroy us, because we believe in them. Remain cool and unruffled so that you can think clearly, size up the challenge accurately and take effective steps to deal with it. This is the way to be superior to the situations of life. This is the way to mobilize the power to deal with every challenge that comes your way. Remain cool and unruffled, no matter what.

It is when the night is darkest that the stars are brightest. There is a precious pearl, a priceless treasure hidden in the depths of your pain, sorrow and adversity. When trouble comes your way, don't let discouragement bury you in its grave. Look up and be inspired by this truth. The stars are brightest when it is darkest. Therefore, it is right there at the end of your road, that your miracle awaits you. Don't give up. Never ever quit. Don't capitalize on the cross lest you crush beneath its weight. Focus on the crown and the cross will become lighter and the road smoother and shorter. Where your mind, heart and soul rest, there your body will be. Keep your eyes on the stars and you'll shine like the stars. Not even the mightiest adversity will be able to overcome you.

It is easy to understand that the lack of clarity about what you truly want, and the absence of a burning desire for what you say you want, is the number one cause of failure. Experience has taught us that if you put all men inside a gold mine, some will come back empty handed, some will come out with a few pieces of gold in their pockets, while some will become millionaires. What you get out of life does not depend on the availability of what you seek, but rather on your *expectation* and *preparation*. Mark these key words. Expectation is the fruit of knowledge, understanding and faith in The Truth. Preparation is how you adapt yourself to be ready to receive in tangible form, the inflow of the Infinite Abundance of life. *Luck* they say, is what happens when opportunity meets with preparation. Most people rely on chance for what they get in life, reason why they easily give up when they come against the slightest roadblock.

Life is an open cheque, given to you to write your own price. Write your price and be sure to get exactly what you've asked for. Set your goals before hand so that when you come upon that master key to all miracles, the world will fail to recognize you, for you would have turned your dreams into reality so fast that even you would be astonished. The laws of nature operate with mathematical accuracy. They are infallible. Like one and one equal two, you will get exactly what you ask for. Ask for a thousand and you'll get a thousand, ask for a million and you'll get a million, ask for a billion and you'll get a billion. Is the picture becoming clearer to you? Stop right here and think. What do you really want? Write it down. Put your dreams – your wildest dreams on paper. Remind yourself that all things will eventually come to you if you know what you truly want and are so committed to it that you will stop at nothing until you have had it.

What would you want to achieve, be, or have by next month, by next year, within the next three, five, ten or twenty years? You must answer this question from the stand point that;

Everyone who seeks, finds
Everyone who asks, receives
Everyone who knocks, the door is opened to him/her
Whatsoever you desire, you attain
Whatsoever you believe, you achieve
Whatsoever you dream, you become.

Yes, all the above affirmations which you will find everywhere in scripture reflect the basic principle of nature that "what you are seeking is already seeking you". If you begin with this premise in mind, everything will change for you. I am out to reveal to you the deep meaning behind these claims – the under currents that animated these words spoken with both power and authority by the masters, prophets and sages of all ages, including Jesus Christ. Nothing is true and useful until it is true and useful to you.

No philosophy or religion, no matter how exalted is worthwhile if it cannot be put into practical application to make your daily living healthier, richer, happier, more peaceful, free and fulfilling. You will not accept that miracles are real, simply because some other fellow is experiencing miracles. You will prove it in your own life. You will awaken the miracle worker within you, and that miracle worker within, will elevate your daily experience into the realm of the miraculous and supernatural. It is there that you'll awaken to the truth that the only life worth living is the life of freedom, success, health, peace, love, happiness and bliss and that this life is for you.

Did you get that? The abundant life is not just for me, your neighbor, your boss, or the fellow seating next to you in church. It is for you as well. You did not come to earth to be a spectator. Everyone has their own play, and you are the protagonist in yours. The difference is that some people know what they want and wake up every morning with the determination and enthusiasm to get what they want, while others rely on chance to bring to them whatsoever is available. Whenever they are faced with a challenge, they call it failure and change their goals.

The belief in failure is usually a reflection of an inner sense of low self-esteem and self-doubt. You do not believe that you deserve the good you desire. You believe that even if you deserve it, there are forces outside of you that are working against you, and so your getting what you want depends on these capricious forces. As a result, even though you may write down your goals, recite your affirmations, and visualize the end result daily, you do not really expect the thing to happen.

But I say to you that which I know for sure; *"The power that governs your life, and the power that will change your life from your present undesirable condition to the life you really want to live, does not lie in any book, the pastor's hands, the doctor's prescription, the 'miracle crusade', the prayers or rituals, your place of birth, where you live, your past experience, your circumstances, your job, your government, your spouse, other people, or any authority".* All these are treasure maps that you can use to find the hidden treasure. But they are not the treasure itself.

Now that you know the places where the key is not found, you will stop looking for it there and concentrate your efforts in the right place. So far you have been fishing for sharks in a muddy pool. No matter how much skill, knowledge and experience you have, these will become useful only when you search for the right thing in the right place. There is a place to turn your single-minded attention to when you go out on that lofty mission of searching for the key to life – the key to all miracles. It is within, not without, that the mystery lies.

He who looks without, dreams; he who looks within, awakens. He, who awakens, has resurrected from the death of poverty, limitation, fear, insecurity, anxiety, frustration, confusion, sickness and misery. He has risen into the glory of the kingdom of freedom, truth, wisdom, love, prosperity, power, wisdom, joy and bliss!

Just as every house stands on a foundation and the survival of that house depends on the strength of its foundation, the life of every entity be it a man, an organization, a system, a religion, a philosophy, a project, a nation, is founded on a certain premise, core value, life principle, foundation truth, hypothesis, or paradigm. Jesus reveals this truth in his metaphor of the man who built his house on solid rock versus the man who built his house on sand.

""Therefore everyone who hears these words of mine and puts them into practice is like a wise man who built his house on the rock. The rain came down, the streams rose, and the winds blew and beat against that house; yet it did not fall, because it had its foundation on the rock. But everyone who

hears these words of mine and does not put them into practice is like a foolish man who built his house on sand. The rain came down, the streams rose, and the winds blew and beat against that house, and it fell with a great crash." (Matthew 7:24-27. NIV).

If your life is founded on a sandy philosophy, everything about you will be shaky and the slightest winds will be enough to tear you apart. It is a tragedy that majority of human beings have more fear than faith, and expect more bad news than good news. This negativity is the very heart of the social conditioning to which we are victims, and those who will free themselves from the chains of this mental enslavement are those who deliberately and consciously do so, by finding the truth and building their lives upon it. "You shall know the truth, and the truth shall set you free."

CHAPTER 9

Expanded Consciousness

The ninth insight:

Ignorance resulting from conditioned consciousness is the root of all fear, stress, hate, disease, poverty, and failure. There is a realm of expanded consciousness beyond the doctrines of our social institutions and physical life. You enter the realm of expanded consciousness by realizing that the conditioned consciousness is false. It is only from the realm of expanded consciousness that you can transform your life.

After helping Ben escape from FBI custody, Ian returns the Declaration and asks for the next clue, but when Ben remains coy, Ian reveals he has kidnapped Patrick as a hostage.

Ian: The Declaration and the Meerschaum Pipe. All yours.
Ben: That's it?
Ian: That's it. I knew you would keep your promise. Now where is it? Where is my treasure?
Ben: It's right here. The map said Heere at the Wall, spelled with two Es. Wall Street follows the path of an actual wall that the Dutch settlers built as a defense to keep the British out. The main gate was located at a street called Deheere, also two Es. Later Deheere was renamed Broadway after the British got in. So Heere at the Wall, Broadway, Wallstreet. Cheerio.
Ian: Just a moment Ben.
Ben: Ian if you break our deal, the FBI will be only a few minutes behind you. You might get away, you might not.
Ian: Is that all the map said?
Ben: Every word.
Ian: Oh Ben you know the key to running a convincing bluff? Every once in a while, you've got to be holding all the cards.
Ben: [realizes Ian has taken his Father hostage]...Dad...!
Ian: Is there anything else you want to tell me?
Ben: Trinity Church. We have to go inside Trinity Church.
Ian: Good. Excellent. Why don't you ask Doctor Chase and Riley to join us? I'm sure they are around here somewhere.

The group travels to the Trinity Church where they find an underground passage. Trinity Church is located on Wall Street and Broadway in New York City. Inside the church they take a look at the map again, using the other lens which Ben had accidentally noticed on the Franklin glasses while handcuffed to the table at the FBI office. The clue revealed from the complete reading of the map leads them through the tomb of a knight (Pakington Lane) into an underground passage with a spiraling staircase.

The location of Trinity Church at the intersection of Wall Street and Broadway is a symbolic representation of reality that there is a place where history, science, capitalism, and religion meet. That meeting place is not inside the church but several stories beneath the church. This is a very important clue. The treasure we seek in life belongs to a different realm than the one our problems are currently occupying. Thus, for our lives to change, we must be ready to transcend our current consciousness and enter the expanded consciousness which Jesus calls heaven. It is only by dying to our current reality that we are born into the new. Success is not about fixing or improving our lives. It is about transforming our lives the way the seed becomes a tree and a caterpillar becomes a butterfly.

The state of consciousness that is creating all our problems is the social conditioning we have received from society. We are the product of the systems of beliefs, dogmas, creeds, laws, cultures, and habits that have been packaged and passed down to us in the form of history, religion, science, economics, government, education, and so on. Those who accept this programmed reality without questioning live in the bliss of ignorance and suffer the misery of a life that is not truly theirs. Freedom begins with the realization that this reality is false. When you awaken from the dream of the false, then you are ready to embrace the truth that lies beneath the veil of appearances.

When you look through a telescope into outer space, you realize that our earth is part of a solar system, our solar system is part of the milky way galaxy, our milky way galaxy is part of a cluster of galaxies, and our cluster is part of a greater whole that is made up of many clusters. In between and beyond the planets, solar systems and galaxies, is space. If you look in the opposite direction with the help of a microscope and particle accelerators you find that every organism is made up of tissues, tissues are assemblies of specialized cells, cells are organized units of chemical reactions, chemical reactions are a systematic exchange of energy between atoms and molecules, atoms are micro-solar systems made up of electrons spinning on an orbit around a central nucleus, and electrons are made up of pockets of light, such as photons. In between and beyond all organisms, cells, atoms, and photons, is space. This brings us to the conclusion that the material universe is a parenthesis hanging in the midst of an infinity of space.

There is now no debate as to whether or not the space in the universe is empty. All of modern science is based on the old assumption that atoms are the building blocks of matter and that there is nothing in the space that links atoms or objects. Recent discoveries have now called that assumption to question, thereby crumbling the very foundation of science itself. There is a Unified Field which matter, biological life, space, and time can all be traced back to. This Unified Field is the generator of all that is, the container of all that is, and the bridge between all that is, because it permeates all that is. There is no scientist who can question the existence of this Unified Field. The only differences in opinion now is on the nature of the Field.

The mere discovery that there is a Unified Field from which all matter, biological life, space, and time emerges and exists, is enough grounds to dismantle the reality that we have built over the centuries. This fact has been known and taught throughout the ages by the spiritual traditions and philosophers, but the scientists, functioning from the materialist paradigm, could not accept it until they could measure it. Now that the Unified Field has been proven scientifically, the science textbooks need to be re-written, and all aspects of modern civilization that were built on the assumption of separateness which science used to uphold, is now up for a reformatting.

Newtonian science championed the paradigm that matter is made up of atoms, that life forms are discrete entities that are separated from each other by space, and that space is 'empty'. This science is the ancestor of all the applied sciences that make up modern civilization; economics, politics, medicine, psychology, education, technology, etc. By disproving all these assumptions of Newtonian science, modern science has proven that all applied sciences are faulty, and humanity has been living a lie. By stretching our knowledge to this new boundary called the Unified Field, we can rewrite the laws governing our health, relationships, careers, finances, business, environment, educational systems, and governments.

Also, physicists are now making the startling discovery that the material universe is the expression of codes or patterns that when reduced to their deepest essence, are found to be actual computer codes. The idea of a coded universe is not at all strange because it is obvious. For biological life, for example, there is a genetic code that defines the kingdom, the genus, the species, and the individual. In our daily lives, we use technologies that are basically computer codes that have been written into a software. Where do you think we got that idea of computer coding from? Is there any logic in thinking that biological life is coded in the form of DNA, and yet the rest of the universe is occurring at random?

Looking at matter we find that the structure of the atom is the same structure of the solar system, and this pattern is repeated in every system in between. It makes sense that all of the universe is the expression of a code. If it were not so, the mango tree in Jamaica would be different from the one in Nigeria and the rock in Gibraltar would be made up of a different stuff from the rock in Cape Town.

Scientists have settled on the idea that we are living in a coded universe. What is keeping people worried now is the implications of this discovery. Are we living in a computer simulation? If yes, whose code are we following? If we are just expressions of a code, do we actually have a life of our own? To say that we are living in a computer simulation will be to use the babbling of a toddler to describe the wisdom of elders. Computers and codes are human language. They are okay as metaphors, but we cannot say that the universe is a computer simulation.

My assertion is that the universe inspired us to invent the computer codes after the pattern through which the universe itself functions. An image is a copy of the object that is projecting the image. If man is the image of God, then man's life should be unfolding after the pattern in which God's life unfolds. We live in an intelligent universe which expresses itself through patterns or codes. The way I see it, the pattern is responsible for the expression of the generic universe of which man is a part. But man is not merely a biological life form like the animals and plants. Man is a spirit clothed in human form. The spirit that man is, is that same Spirit that is the intelligent universe, such that man is the individualization or Image or Son of that Intelligence. Man, therefore lives in a coded universe in which he is a co-creator.

This being the case, it becomes evident that man is the microcosm of the macrocosm called the universe. That is, the spirit of man and his human body corresponds to the Infinite Spirit and its body called Creation. The purpose of human life is the replication, on an individualized scale, of the Universal Creative Principle that brings forth the generic universe. This specialization of the law leads to the creation of an infinite variety of experiences. Infinite self-expression is the counterpart of the Infinite Potentiality that the Unified Field is. So, as the theologians put it, "the glory of God is man fully alive".

From the most basic atomic structure, through complex biological life, up to the galaxies and beyond, we find that reality is a spiral of universes existing within universes, and worlds existing within worlds. The basic stuff out of which all things are made is energy, and this creative energy has been found to be intelligent, and in a state of constant vibration. Intelligence implies intention. Nothing happens at random. Randomness appears only to the human mind which cannot comprehend the intelligence behind the seeming randomness. Vibration implies frequencies. Each range of frequencies of the vibration of Source Energy accounts for a kingdom of life forms or level of existence. Thus, we have the mineral world, the plant world, the animal kingdom, the mental world, and the spirit world.

Within each world, the sub-frequencies define the individuals, and individual frequencies interact in a network of like frequencies to form a matrix. If we understand this basic notion that we are spiritual beings living in a spiritual universe and that our conscious activity defines our frequency of vibration, it becomes obvious that what we call our reality at any given moment, is a field of energy that has been created by the intertwining of our energy frequency with the energy frequencies of those who are at the same level of vibration with us. This frequency network or energy field is what we may call a matrix. There are therefore countless matrices in the universe, the lower frequencies living within the higher frequencies on a continuum.

In the book of Genesis, we are presented with a metaphor of this ascending scale of energy frequencies. Jacob places his head on a stone (as his pillow) and falls asleep. In his sleep, he has a dream in which the gate of heaven opens, and he sees a stairway leading from him right to heaven, with God at the other end, and there are angels ascending and descending. The stone represents the earth, matter, the mineral kingdom, which is the grossest form of life or the lowest frequency of vibration. The Lord at the end of the stairway in heaven represents the Source Energy, the Creator or Father from which all things proceed, in which all things exist, and to whom all things return. The stairway with angels ascending and descending represents the spiral of consciousness, each step standing for a level of awareness. Angels are spiritual messengers or the energy of God, hence the angels in this dream symbolize the states of consciousness that man occupies and defines his life by.

The lower our state of consciousness or frequency of vibration, the closer we are to matter or the stone. The higher our consciousness or frequency of vibration, the closer we are to the God State. Lower frequencies are always under the command or control of higher frequencies. Those who are at a lower state of consciousness are forever under the spell of those who are functioning at a higher state of consciousness. Each step on that spiritual ladder, each level of consciousness, is therefore a matrix, that is linked with the matrix below it and the matrix above it, by the ladder of conscious evolution. Man has the power and freedom to move up and down the ladder as he pleases, by altering his own awareness.

The material universe is an infinitesimally tiny parenthesis existing within the Infinity of Space that gives rise to it, contains it, and sustains it. This Space is a Living Presence which intentionally unfolds the created universe as its self-expression, following specific patterns, codes, or laws that are visible in the world of form. Man's physical body is part of the generic creation, but his essence which is spirit, is one with the Infinite Intelligence.

Man, therefore is the Infinite Intelligence, individualizing himself, so that through the platform of individuality or free will, he may replicate the Universal Creative Principle that brings forth the generic universe, thereby creating an infinite variety of specialized experiences. Because man is a being with a dual nature - a spirit living in a body, his experience of life is a result of the quality of his awareness. He who is aware of himself as a purely physical being represents the stone at the foot of the ladder in Jacob's dream; he who is aware of himself as a purely spiritual being represents the Lord at the top of the ladder in Jacob's dream; in between these two extremes is the ascending spiral of levels of consciousness or matrices that define the reality of human existence.

With this evidence that we have expounded upon, with that truth that appears so obvious that we now wonder how come we haven't thought of it before, I therefore, exhort you to wake up to the fact that you are not your mind, your body, your circumstances – that these are merely experiences that you are having, and these experiences account for less than 0.1% of physical reality. If this is true for the material universe then it must be true for the whole universe including the immaterial universe. The realms of matter, the electromagnetic spectrum, electricity, and gravitation, are the realms that we have been able to measure so far with our equipment.

The boundaries of science have been pushed to the quantum field, and beyond the quantum field there are even higher frequencies of vibration. Thought and emotion are vibrations that exist beyond this quantum level. Clinical studies can now measure brain waves and heart waves, so this too is no longer a matter of speculation. Thought and emotion produce energy waves that can be measured clinically. There are normal frequency ranges for the different biological brain states, but it has been proven that in altered states of consciousness the brain waves emit frequencies that are off the charts. In my opinion, these clinically measurable brain and heart waves are not thoughts and emotions in themselves, but the electromagnetic energy emitted by the physical brain and heart in response to the impulse of thought and emotion on them. Thoughts and feelings themselves are not yet directly measurable. Their measurement is indirect, through their effect on matter.

The whole point of this exposé is to engrave upon your awareness the rock-solid conviction that we live in a universe that is One, Infinite, and Conscious. This Infinite Oneness constitutes an Infinite Sea of Possibility, from which we "harvest" our personal reality using the measure of what we accept as real (in other words, our beliefs). Finally, you can transform your life deliberately, based on knowledge. This faith is the substance that constitutes the real source of riches. When you are immersed in this state, anything you set your hands to do becomes a spontaneous outlet of prosperity. When you live in the Awareness of Infinite Supply, you are rich. What you do, becomes the expression of this richness that you are, and money flows effortlessly and inevitably in response to this state of being.

Begin by realizing the basic law of your being: "You are Energy or Spirit. Spirit is in perpetual vibration. Attention is the directing power of Vibrating Spirit or Consciousness. Where attention goes, energy flows. Hence where your attention is, you are".

✓ Take your attention away from the circumstances that surround you.
✓ Take your attention away from your mind and body.

✓ Place your attention on the Reality that is Omnipresent, Omnipotent, Omniscient; the Universal I AM that is All Love, All Wisdom, All Power, All Substance.

✓ Then recognize that this All Loving, All Powerful, All Wise, Absolute, Eternal, and Infinite I AM, is the I AM that I AM (the I AM that YOU ARE)

Make it a habit to do this exercise as naturally and in as relaxed a mood as you can every day, and keep doing it till you catch the Feeling of I AM THAT I AM.

When you catch the FEELING, it is your indication, your proof or confirmation that I AM THAT I AM has ceased to be just a mental affirmation but is now a vital reality in your being. You have experienced the Shift, the Birth from Above, the Awakening or the Transformation. The Secret is to give so much attention to this feeling that you make it as tangible as possible, so that you will be able to invoke it at will, any time you want to enter into the Secret Place. You will eventually get to the place where this awareness is more real to you than the report of your senses, and you will live your life naturally from it.

The in-rushing of the Spirit during Worship, Prayer, or flights of Inspiration comes as Ecstasy or a Rapture. It is easy to recognize the Feeling of God if you have ever felt any of these. The Feeling of God, the I AM THAT I AM Feeling, is the Feeling of Peace, Love, Ecstasy. On the other hand, you can use external triggers to this feeling such as your love relationships, contemplating nature, music/dance, playing your favorite sports, worship, etc. When you use these external triggers to create this feeling, you can then impregnate this feeling with the Conscious Awareness of the Presence of God, and the Conscious Recognition of this Presence of God as the I AM that you ARE.

The I AM is the real you. The *conditioned self* is not the real self but rather the experience of the real self. You are God experiencing himself in this point in time and space as the human being called you. The human is God's faculty of volition, selection, or free will, inserted within the Infinite Oneness for the purpose of specializing the Generic Creative Principle in the universe into an infinite variety of experiences. Self-consciousness is the Nature of the Divine Spirit, and man is self-conscious, reason why he is called the Image of God.

Realize your *sublime self* and enthrone it as master over your sentient self and all physical reality. The Christ Life, the Word by which all the worlds are formed is Pure Unconditioned Love pouring from the bosom of God into expression. It is your self-reflection that conditions this Light into the conditions you are experiencing. You do not make the river of life to flow. The Flow is the reason why you are alive so all you need to do is align yourself with it by Consciously Acknowledging It and employing your *free will* to control your *imagination* and *attention* so that you present to this life force only blueprints (images) of that which you really want to be – that which corresponds to your highest good and that of all.

Paint a picture of your ideal self, surrounded by the best conditions you can imagine for your life; the money, the home, the cars, the clothes, the employment/business, the community service, etc. anything that appeals to your fancy, that awakens your passion, and that gives you the best feeling of aliveness, of joy, of blessedness, of increasing life to humanity. When your goal resonates with your heart energy (love), then you won't need any effort to stay focused on it. The attention is always where the heart is. The Energy doesn't care how you condition it. Free Will is your ultimate gift. But since it is a universe of Law, the only condition is that you will pay for every choice you make. If your goals are inspired by self-gratification and turn you into an agent of evil, you will not escape your reward. If your goals as inspired by love and the desire for increasing life for all and the glory of God, you too, will not escape your reward.

Beyond that, the Energy does not care. If you condition it as a dollar, a steady stream of billions of dollars, freedom to move around and enjoy all the goodness of nature, a palace, an empire, a private jet, a university, a new city, a new ideal of human government, a cure for some killer disease, a solution to climate change, …so long as you are definite in your goal (free will), bring it to the feeling level of passion in your heart (attention), and hold the image of its fulfillment in your consciousness (imagination) as you enter and dwell in the Presence daily; so long as you do this, nothing in heaven or earth can stop you from getting what you want.

CHAPTER 10

The Dark Night of The Soul

The tenth insight:

Just as dawn is preceded by midnight, just as the germination of a new plant is preceded by the death of the seed, just as the birth of the butterfly is preceded by the death of the caterpillar, the finding of the treasure of life is preceded by a dead end, a Calvary experience, or what is often termed the dark night of the soul. It is out of this darkness that the new self emerges.

The search team reaches a dead end at the foot of the spiraling staircase, lit by a lantern. In order to evade death, Patrick tells Ian that the lantern is another clue. Ian and his team leave Ben and his team trapped in the cave beneath Trinity Church and head for Boston following the fake clue that Patrick has given them.

Patrick Gates: *It's part of Freemason teachings. In King Solomon's temple there was a winding staircase. It signified the journey that had to be made to find the light of truth. The lantern is the clue.*
Ian: *What does it mean?*
Ben: *Boston. It's Boston.*
Patrick Gates: *The Old North Church, where Thomas Newton hung a lantern in the steeple, to signal Paul Revere that the British were coming. One if by land, two if by sea. One lantern. Under the winding staircase of the steeple, that's where we have to look.*
Ian: *Thank you.*
Patrick Gates: *Hey, you have to take us with you.*
Ian: *Why? So, you can escape in Boston? Besides, with you out of the picture, there's less baggage to carry.*
Patrick Gates: *What if we lied?*
Ian: *Did you?*
Ben: *What if there's another clue?*
Ian: *Then I'll know right where to find you. See you, Ben.*
[Ian and his team of mercenaries depart leaving Ben, Patrick, Abigail, and Riley trapped in the dead end five stories beneath Trinity Church]

Ben, Patrick, Abigail, and Riley are trapped in the underground cave while Ian and his men leave for Boston to pursue the lead that Patrick has given them. But Abigail knows her history well:

Abigail: *Alright boys what's going on? The British came by sea. It was two lanterns not one.*

Patrick: *Ian needed another clue, so we gave it to him.*
Riley: *It was fake. It was a fake clue.*

Meanwhile, Ben is not part of the conversation. His mind is working. He is scanning the seeming bare walls very intently. Something catches his attention:

Ben: *The all-seeing eye. Through the all-seeing eye.*
Riley: *That means by the time Ian figures it out, we'll still be trapped down here, and he will shoot us then. Either way we're going to die.*
Ben: *Nobody is going to die. There is another way out.*
Riley: *Where?*
Ben: *Through the treasure room.*

The All-Seeing-Eye symbol on the wall turns out to be the key to a secret passage way as Ben had suspected. He opens it, and it leads them into the actual treasure room.

When you sow a seed into the ground there is a period of darkness and silence during which the seed dies in order for the tree within it to germinate. In the life of a caterpillar, there is a period of pupation, a darkness and silence during which the caterpillar dies in order for the butterfly to emerge from it. The dead end that Ben faces here is not just failure. It is actually the end. The final clue has led him through a tomb in a church, down a spiraling staircase to the belly of the earth. The treasure is nowhere to be found, and Ian has left him there for death. Even if he wanted to give up and go home, he couldn't.

This is the end, not just for the treasure hunt, but for his life. What Ben is experiencing here is what the mystics call "the dark night of the soul". It is often characterized by extreme spiritual torture. The world you used to know crashes at your feet, you question your very existence, you question the existence of God, you think to the limits of thinking, and feel pain to the limits of feeling, and you just blank out.

The good news is that the dark night of the soul is actually a signal that the new you is about to be born. The dark night of the soul is the midnight that announces the dawn, or the labor pains that announces the arrival of a new baby. There is no way you can experience the new birth without passing through the dark night of the soul. And there is no way you can experience the dark night of the soul and not resurrect as a new luminous being. Unfortunately, most humans never descend to such depths of experience because they are busy with the superficial quests that fetch them the crumbs of life.

This new reality that is about to be born is the true self that you came to earth to become, the light that the world has been waiting for. Question is, do you even realize that your present self is like a caterpillar compared to the butterfly that you are here to become? Do you realize that the only reason why you are contented with your life as it is because you have no clue about your life as it can be?

There are two kingdoms in this world, the kingdom of the gods and the kingdom of mere men. We all walk around in the same human form, but we are not all the same. Some are masters, prophets, geniuses, kings and queens, while others are slaves who may not know it, but are spending all their days at the service of the masters. Success is a word that has been greatly abused in this century, yet few know what success really is. Many church folks have been accused of preaching a so-called "prosperity gospel" yet very few know what prosperity really is about.

People have claimed that they have found their purpose here on earth and may go about enjoying this masquerade dance we have created with the illusion that they are experiencing self-fulfillment. The most exalted level of success in the kingdom of men is like a grain of sand on the shores of the gods. The gods speak not in terms of achieving success, prosperity, wealth, abundance, health, fame, fortune, and influence. The gods think and speak only in terms of being who they are – gods, because all these things are inherent in their nature. They wake up every day just to experience in a variety of ways, that which they already are.

"Know you not that you are gods, sons of the Most-High?" I can imagine the tone of voice the master used as he tried to stir his listeners up from sleep. I can imagine his frustration after spending his whole ministry trying to reveal to man his true self and yet finding his very own disciples insisting on remaining mere men. Oh, I may have doubted these words if it was my grandfather who had uttered them. But no, they were spoken from the lips of God Himself while he walked the earth in the person of Jesus the Messiah. You are all gods and goddesses. All of you are sons and daughters of the Most-High. You ought to be living here as princes and princesses of heaven, heirs and heiresses of the fullness of God, yet you have chosen to die like mere men. How sad!

The universe is groaning as with the pangs of childbirth, awaiting the manifestation of the sons of God. This world we live in is an incubator, a womb, whose purpose and only desire is to nurture the men – the gods-in-embryo that are born into this material existence till they experience their second birth as gods and begin blessing the world with the miracles of their divine nature.

The human life you are living is not your real life. It is the embryonic form of your real life. No matter how intelligent and civilized man has become, no matter how impressive his inventions, his economic and government systems, even his philosophies and religions, the achievements of mere men are mere dust on the ground upon which the gods walk. Only the gods are truly alive. Only the gods are authentic beings. The universe's only purpose is to give birth to the gods that will manifest the glory of God. The only purpose of life on earth is to give birth to the real you. The self you now carry is a mere seed. It is not the real you. All your experiences, all that you have been through and will ever go through are leading you to the one miraculous moment when you are truly born – when the god in you becomes manifest. The question is "do you choose to be born again?"

We must fix firmly in our minds this idea of Life as the spontaneous, unconditional, and perpetual outpouring of All-that-is from Infinity into expression through us, in us, and as us. If we realize that this current of Love or Grace is the law of our being, that it is divine mechanics that we have nothing to do about, many things change in our lives automatically:

Firstly, we come into the conscious realization that it is Life that is living us, not us living life; it is God who is loving us, not us loving God; it is our good that is seeking us, not us seeking our good. Did you just get the sensation of a burden being lifted off your shoulders? All our struggles, failures, and pain are the result of the false assumption that we are in charge, that it is us that are making life happen, that there is a white bearded man in some far off heaven who is a *rewarder* of those who obey his commandments and punisher of those who do not; that the universe is static and hostile to us, and we only get what we need to survive by undertaking religious transactions with this far off God, and sharp economic transactions with the world around us.

You are an emanation of All-that-is, living and moving and having your being in the All-that-is, which is also living and moving and having Its being in you, through you, and as you. You are Love seeking expression; You are Abundance seeking manifestation; You are Power seeking activity. When we learn to "be still and know that I AM", we allow this current of Love, this Breath of God to be through us that which it is through the sun, moon, and stars; that which it is through the roses and waterfalls: the spontaneous, unconditional, and perpetual outpouring of life in all its fullness.

Secondly, we recognize the falseness in the assumption that we are beings that are separate from God, the Universe and one another. It is this false assumption of separateness that makes us believe that that which we want is somewhere out there caring less about us, and we need to do something in order to coerce and attract it into our lives. If the very livingness of God is the spontaneous, unconditional, and perpetual outpouring into glorious self-expression in us, through us, as us, then it goes without saying that all that is, all that has ever been, and all that will ever be, exists for us, is in love with us, and is eternally seeking us even as the river is eternally flowing into the sea.

Thirdly, we come to the conclusion that time and space (past-present-future, here-there, big-small) is not a concrete force on which our reality depends, but rather a three-dimensional screen on which we experience the realities we have created in our awareness. Infinite Consciousness is the Ultimate Reality, and Infinite Consciousness is All-that-is, the Field of Infinite Possibilities in which all things simultaneously exist in the eternal now. Time is the dance of the waves upon this Infinite Ocean of Motion in which all possibilities are contained, and our being is this dance. When we understand this truth, we immediately come to the realization that the memories and fears by which we enslave ourselves are fictitious. The past and future as we know them, do not exist.

You are the Eternal Self that exists beyond time and space and generates through self-awareness, your experience of self, on the disc of your consciousness. Your brain is the projector through which you project this movie on the screen of space-time, and your bodily senses are the mechanism through which you experience this self-created movie. Knowing that all space-time experience is but a mind movie, and that the reality is the timeless self-awareness you are having within, you can freely and joyfully create new experiences to replace the ones that do not serve you.

The conviction that the Universe is for you, in you, and with you is the foundation of Faith. Here faith is resolved into the illumination of the consciousness with the light of Truth thereby setting the individual free from the beliefs and conditionings that had cast his/her life into bondage. Indeed "you shall know that truth, and the truth shall set you free".

You are the breath of God, clothed in the image and likeness of God, living and moving and having your being in the garden of God, and blossoming into the glory of God. If only we recognized in every person the flowering of God, every human encounter would be an act of worship. Genius is what you are naturally; Power is what you are naturally;

An orange seed does not need to do anything in order to become an orange seed. It is an orange seed by the mere fact of its being. Man is divinity-in-embryo. Man is Infinite Potentiality encapsulated in a human form. The orange seed fulfills its purpose (attains greatness) by unfolding the orange nature within itself. Man fulfills his potential (attains greatness) by recognizing and unfolding the divine nature within himself. Genius is what you are, by virtue of being human. Greatness is what you become, by virtue of letting your genius express itself.

The people we call "Stars" are people who have found their inner genius and are living from it, not necessarily in the holistic way we demonstrated in the success code, but at least in the aspect that has brought them to prominence. You have not yet found yours because you are too busy looking at them and trying to be like them. When you find your inner genius and live from it, you will be a miracle worker on this earth, and there will be no competition for you. The problem you are capable of perceiving is the problem you are capable of solving. You did not come here to be a victim. You are here to be a solution to the problems your world is facing. If you pay attention to the challenges that come your way, you will find in them hints of your calling, and the key to unlocking your genius.

What Jesus said "I and my Father are one" is true as well for anyone who professes to be a child of God. So, don't look for God in strange places or spectacular prophesies from some folks you think are more anointed than you are. The greatest miracle of all is the realization that God is eternally in you, with you, for you, and through you. If only you knew what you could become, you will never for a single moment be contented with what you have become. It doesn't matter if you have sinned or failed to the degree that you have become the gate keeper of hell. When the Christ in you awakens, that Father that is within as you, will transform even that hell into a heaven.

You are a special gift to this universe. There is a unique potential in you that once unraveled and expressed will be a blessing to the world. Your presence here is a promise from God that things are about to get better for the world around you, and you are the channel through which this miracle will happen. No one can sing your song. No one can dance your dance. Only you can fill your place in this life, and the kingdom will be incomplete if you die with your music inside of you.

The farmer does not fast, pray, visualize, and perform a whole lot of psychological and religious gymnastics, for stems, leaves, and fruits to fly out of the sky and stick themselves to the mango seed so as to make it a tree. No. He simply plants his seed in the soil, knowing that the mango tree is contained in the seed - trunk, branches, leaves, fruits, and more seeds. He knows as a matter of fact that his seed will germinate and unfold the potentialities it contains, and in due season he will have a mango tree laden with fruit. What we call faith, belief, trust, etc is simply the positive awareness that you are a divine ideal in seed form, and that all that you require to unfold into the highest potential you are capable of, is already yours. Yes, the kingdom of heaven is within you, waiting for you to shape it into any manifestation you desire. The question is, will you?

When you choose to rise above the mundane life you have been programmed to live, and seek the hidden treasures of life, you will come to a point on your journey where your whole life is disrupted like a hurricane has swept over you. Do not be afraid. The old must be demolished in order for the new to be built. Hang on just a while longer, and your new dawn will break forth in ways you could never have imagined.

CHAPTER 11

Behold The Treasure

The eleventh insight:

In the very moment when you feel like fainting, in the very instant where you feel like your night is at its darkest, in that very experience when you feel like you are in the belly of hell itself, it is there that you will find the treasure you have been seeking. Your life story, no matter how tragic, is the container of your gift. Look for it and you will find it.

Well, they are now in the treasure room, but there is no treasure here. What the hell is going on? Did someone find the treasure before them a long time ago? They are certain that this is the treasure room. All the clues have led to this. But where is the treasure?

Ben is frustrated, and confesses that Patrick had been right all along that the treasure was fiction. But Patrick has had a change of mind. He reassures Ben that all evidence in that room pointed to the fact that the treasure was reality. Someone had simply moved it before they had gotten here. Patrick praises Ben's skills and reassures him that to have deciphered all the clues that led to this room, meant that he was extraordinarily gifted. Patrick tells Ben he is proud of him. They hug each other and reconcile.

Ben: I just really thought I was going to find the treasure.
Patrick: Okay, then we just keep on looking for it.
Abigail: I'm in.
Ben: Okay
Riley: Not to be Johnny rain cloud, but that's not going to happen. Because as far as I can see, we're still trapped down here. Oh Ben where's this other way out?
Ben: Well, that's it. It doesn't make sense. The first thing the builders would have done after getting down here was cut a secondary shaft back for air...
Patrick: Right
Ben: ... in case of cave ins. Could it be that simple? The secret lies with Charlotte.

While speaking and fidgeting on the walls, Ben's renewed inspiration leads him to uncover a notch which the meerschaum pipe fits into, opening a large chamber, and behold, there lies the treasure.

Ben contacts Sadusky, surrendering the Declaration and the treasure's location in exchange for clemency. He requests that the finding of the treasure should be credited to the entire Gates family, with the help of Riley. It turns out that Sadusky is actually a Freemason, as indicated by the ring on his finger. Sadusky and Ben discuss the idea that the reason why the founding fathers hid these treasures was because they were too immense to be owned by one person. Like the government, the treasure belongs to the people. So, they decided to return the treasure to the people by distributing it to various museums around the world. Ian is later arrested when Ben tips the FBI off.

He who has found the hidden treasure has become a new creation. "I tell you most solemnly. No man can enter the kingdom of heaven unless he is born again." This is the hallmark of life, explicitly taught by Christianity and every other great religion. Man's ultimate quest is the kingdom of heaven, and there is no other way he can enter that kingdom unless he is "born again". Where most religions and philosophies differ from one another is what they interpret "the kingdom of heaven" and "born again" to mean. He who has experienced the truth first hand has the liberty and power to "teach with authority", so I will not refer you to any religious teaching or philosophical treatise on the issue but will tell what I know to be the truth about the matter from experience. When you have your own encounter with truth, you will know.

The kingdom of heaven is the spiritual dimension of life in which man is at one with God. Here man lives and moves and has his being in God, while God lives and moves and has His being in man, through man, and as man. *The father in me and I in the father.* The kingdom of heaven is not some geographical location in time and space to which we earn an entry visa after death based on the record of good and religiousness we have accumulated. It is a state of being that we enter beginning from the moment we are born again and stretching into eternity with ever ascending levels of glory as portrayed by Jacob's ladder at Bethel.

To enter this kingdom where all the treasures of life are stored up, there is only one way. You must be born again. Now to be born again is not the ceremonial public confession and baptism that our churches have made a show of. It is not to quit your traditional church and go looking for a Pentecostal so called "spirit filled Bible believing church". Words do not make a thing so. Confessing or affirming that "I am swimming" does not make you swim. No less does claiming "I am born again" make you born again. Man is a spiritual being having a human experience. His state of consciousness defines his identity and reality. Life is a spiritual evolution in which through experience man grows to catch a glimpse of his divine self beyond the human self and thereby experiences a metamorphosis or change of state.

The man who identifies with the human self is the sinner, the Adam, the fallen being who is ruled by the evidence of the senses. The man who identifies with the divine self is the righteous one, the Christ, the resurrected being who reigns through faith. The transition from the human-consciousness to the spirit-consciousness, the passage from the Adam-identity to the Christ-identity, the translation from the kingdom of mere men to the kingdom of the gods, is what it means to be born again. This is the finding of the hidden treasure.

Life is a spiritual evolution, or the evolution of consciousness. We are travelling from the world of forgetfulness to the world of knowing; from the state of sleep to the state of wakefulness; from the name Jacob to the name Israel. The universe is our incubator, the arena of self-discovery through experience. The human self, made up of body, mind, and soul is the vessel that the spirit self uses to navigate this space-time sphere of experience. When we are first born, we are not aware that we are spirit beings.

Our first encounter is with our bodies and environment, then we grow to master the mind, and then the soul. The first phase of our life on earth is the development and perfection of this vessel, this human self to make it ready for use by the spirit. But most often, once we have perfected our muscles and looks, our brains and wits, and even our souls, we get so impressed that we are mesmerized into the belief that this is all there is. We go to church, engage in good deeds, fast and pray, and rest assured that we are heaven bound. But that is just the ripening of the seed.

The second phase of life is the birth of the spirit or divine self, the resurrection of the Christ identity upon the death of the Adam identity. To know yourself as a mere human is to be Adam. To know yourself as divine – Son of the Most-High, is to be Christ. The birth of the spirit is therefore a shift in consciousness from human awareness to divine awareness. This happens when you awaken to the falseness of the false. It's the same mechanism that happens when you are experiencing a nightmare.

The moment you remember that it is just a nightmare, you awaken from it into the relief or reality. So, when you go through the nightmare of ordinary human life, the role of all your experiences is to bring you to that crucial moment of remembering that this is just a nightmare – a false reality.

When you recognize the false as false, then the false disappears and the truth takes its place. The truth has always been there, you are not creating it. It has always been lying behind the veil of sense consciousness that you were fixated to. The moment you realize that the veil is a lie, it disappears and the light of truth takes its place. As depicted by the National Treasure, the great institutions, beautiful streets, and busy lifestyles we have built to keep us occupied are standing on a treasure that generations upon generations trample underfoot without a clue that such a treasure even exists.

You are here today, reading this book because it is your time to awaken and join the company of the gods. If not so, this book wouldn't have found its way to you. The birthing forth of the god in you is an internal affair. Humans are fanatics of rituals and entertainment. You may go through them if you choose, but keep in mind that the merit is not in the outer words and actions but in the spirit they symbolize. "The letter kills; It is the spirit that gives life". You do not need to change your church. What needs changing is your mentality, your inner spirit. When you are born again, when you become a citizen of the kingdom of the gods – the kingdom of heaven, you become a master over the earth. You exercise a miraculous power over everything material or mental be it your health, relationships, occupation and finances, or those of those you care about.

Ben used to be a subject of public ridicule. You would recall that when he went to the National archives to see Doctor Chase, he could not afford to use his real name. His family name was despised by the academic community because their belief and search for the National Treasure defied the orthodoxy of education, religion, politics, and tradition. But when this broke, unpopular, unloved fellow found the National Treasure, he stumbled on a wealth so great that it could not be held by one institution or one country. In that instant, his life experienced a quantum leap to wealth, power, and greatness. Success and riches became child's play. Now that is what I call transformation.

When you find the hidden treasure, you begin to play by a different set of rules and reign over the lower laws of the lower worlds. That is why they, the mere men will begin giving you names. Did you get that? They will know that you belong to a different dimension of life and will flock to you, calling you names and seeking to worship you. But that will not be your interest, because love will be your only song, and helping others awaken will be your only job.

Welcome to your domain oh blessed one. Happy birthday to you, divine son of the Most-High. Here in the father's house are many mansions; enter into yours. The fattened calf has been slaughtered and a feast has been prepared for you. Come let us eat, drink, dance and make merry. As we celebrate the glory of life, and our splendor bathes the earth we will stir the souls of men and one by one they too will awaken to populate heaven.

It doesn't matter what it is you are seeking. Whether it is love and relationship, physical healing, career and financial success, freedom, and peace of mind... whatever it is you are seeking, the first step toward attaining it is the realization that the only place where you will ever find it is within you, for it is within you that the secret lies; it is within you that the kingdom of heaven dwells, as you. With Faith (Awakened Awareness) you plug into the infinite sea of substance in which is found all life, love, wisdom, power, and all the fullness of God; With the Imagination you create the picture of what you want to experience in your physical life; With your actions you create the channels through which your good will flow to you.

You have no idea of what you are capable of becoming, because that which lies within you is far beyond your comprehension. That is why the law of life is Faith, not Reason. Dream it, believe it, reach out for it, and you will achieve it. The grain of corn that is sown into the ground contains within itself that mysterious intelligence by which it effortlessly and selectively draws to itself all the elements it needs from the earth to germinate, grow, and blossom with fruit. You too are a seed planted by the Creator in the garden of life. The power to achieve your destiny and ascend to heights of glory, lies within you, waiting for you to awaken to it, through awareness.

In the beginning, there was only God in Spirit form. Then that Spirit became Man. God lives and moves and has His Being in Man, through

Man, as Man; even as Man lives and moves and has his being from God, in God, and for God. Man is the image, likeness, expression, or manifestation of Spirit. You are a spiritual being having a human experience, not a human being having a spiritual experience. The moment you grasp this truth, everything changes.

Knowing and affirming that water will quench your thirst is not enough. You must actually drink the water. Believing and confessing your salvation, healing, or prosperity is only one part. You must live what you believe. Wake up each day with a resolution to do something that will make your today better than your yesterday. The ocean is never too full of water. The heart is never too full of love. Love is the stuff you are made of, so don't be afraid to give it away. There will always be more than enough for anyone who comes your way. Where does the light of the sun come from? What does it mean that "you are the light of the world"? The splendor of the sun is nothing compared to the splendor that is within you. The purpose of this book, this journey, is to help you unlock that inner splendor.

The universe is forever expanding; The universe is forever progressive; Life is ever enlarging; Reality is perpetually evolving; God is always doing a new thing; Every new moment is a miracle waiting to be born. Greatness is what you are naturally. It is not something you achieve. Realize that you were born great. Then get to work and release the greatness that is in you. It is within you that the kingdom of heaven is found, and not in some far off country or planet. If you find the kingdom in you, you will find it everywhere else. If you don't find it in you, you won't find it anywhere else.

What makes an orange seed is the life of the orange within it. An orange seed becomes an orange tree by unfolding the life within it. What you are looking for is wrapped up within you. You are a seed of the divine that is here to unfold. We were all born to shine like the stars do. It baffles the mind how you can assume that the stars in the skies, the birds in the air, and the lilies in the garden are more valuable to the Creator than you. Let the splendor around you serve as a constant reminder that you are here to thrive. I cannot stop these words from pouring out. I am not sure I even know where they are coming from. When you are in your flow, life becomes easier than breathing.

The practical person says the business of life is to earn as many of the good things of the world as the strength of his muscles and the sweat of his brow can afford. The mystic says the business of life is to recognize and dwell in the Divine Presence in every moment. But we are not called to be EITHER practitioners OR mystics; we should be both. Ben's experience teaches us that to live life to the full, we must be practical mystics. Life's only reward is to have lived it to the full. To live life to the full is to give the fire within us the room to burn and shine. This fire is God Himself, therefore making us reservoirs of infinite life, love, goodness, wisdom, and power. What does it matter whether we succeed or fail? Whether we laugh or cry? Whether we live in mansions or under the shade of a tree? No, nothing else matters when we grasp the magic of the heaven within us and concern ourselves with living from this heaven awareness.

If you fill your kitchen sink with water, and then open the cork, you will notice that the water moves down the drain in the form of a spiral or vortex. The vortex is caused by the fact that a smaller hole of identical nature (the outlet), has been created within a bigger hole (the sink). The power of the vortex is not generated by the hole, but rather by the original body of water in the sink. Thus, the larger the sink and the greater the volume of the water in the sink, the greater the vortex.

Extrapolating this phenomenon to the field of Consciousness, we see that there is a Source Field in which we live and move and have our being. Man is the individualization of this Source Field. This relationship between Source and Individuality generates a force that gives rise to a vortex of energy the same way a vortex of water is created in a kitchen sink. The same principle applies in the formation of tornados and hurricanes. To help you have a direct experience of this phenomenon, please endeavor to perform the experiment yourself in your kitchen sink. Alternatively, use the internet to search for satellite videos of the movement of recently ended Hurricane Irma. The vortex is the fullness of the Infinite, flowing toward and through the individual. It immediately becomes clear to us that we as humans are not generators of power, but rather channels of power. The second implication is that Life in its infinite, unconditioned aspect is seeking expression and fulfillment through us. Thus, it is not us that are seeking our good. Rather, it is our good that is seeking us.

By simply observing what happens in your kitchen sink, you can uncover a great mystery about how the universe works, and by implication unveil one of the greatest secrets ever revealed to humankind, a secret capable of turning you into a god on this earth. Imagine what will happen in your life if you really knew that;

- It is not you that is wanting money; it is money that is wanting you,
- It is not you that is seeking love; it is love that is seeking you,
- It is not you that is asking for a job; it is your dream job that is asking for you,
- It is not you that is praying for healing; it is healing that is praying to manifest itself through you?

Could this principle be what Jesus was referring to when he said about the man born blind, *"Neither this man nor his parents sinned," said Jesus, "but this happened so that the works of God might be displayed in him." (cf. John 9:2-3. NIV)*?

In many places in the bible, this principle is revealed, but we simply ignore it:

We love because he first loved us (1 John 4:19. NIV).

Before they call I will answer; while they are still speaking I will hear. (Isaiah 65:24. NIV).

"Do not be afraid, little flock, for your Father has been pleased to give you the kingdom." (Luke 12:32. NIV).

It is God loving us, that creates in us the response of loving God in return. It is God giving himself to us, that creates in us the response of wanting to receive from him. The life of man exists within the life of God; thus, man is the recipient and channel of life, not the generator of life. The wrongful interpretation of the invitation in Matthew 7:7-8 (NIV) is one of the explanations for modern man's fall from grace. The text reads;

"Ask and it will be given to you; seek and you will find; knock and the door will be opened to you. For everyone who asks

receives; he who seeks finds; and to him who knocks, the door will be opened".

But there is a bigger picture that we have ignored for the two thousand years since these words were spoken. This verse is not an invitation to ask for our daily bread, seek our life partner, and knock on the doors of our dream job. It is clearly stated that those who worry about these material things are the pagans. This verse is the continuation of a discourse that Jesus is giving to his followers, beginning in Chapter six of this gospel of Matthew. It is in this same discourse that he teaches about the character of fasting and alms giving, gives us the Lord's prayer, and exhorts us against worrying about material things. Here is an excerpt:

"Therefore, I tell you, do not worry about your life, what you will eat or drink; or about your body, what you will wear. Is not life more than food, and the body more than clothes? Look at the birds of the air; they do not sow or reap or store away in barns, and yet your heavenly Father feeds them. Are you not much more valuable than they? Can any one of you by worrying add a single hour to your life? And why do you worry about clothes? See how the flowers of the field grow. They do not labor or spin. Yet I tell you that not even Solomon in all his splendor was dressed like one of these. If that is how God clothes the grass of the field, which is here today and tomorrow is thrown into the fire, will he not much more clothe you—you of little faith? So, do not worry, saying, 'What shall we eat?' or 'What shall we drink?' or 'What shall we wear?' For the pagans run after all these things, and your heavenly Father knows that you need them. But seek first his kingdom and his righteousness, and all these things will be given to you as well. Therefore, do not worry about tomorrow, for tomorrow will worry about itself. Each day has enough trouble of its own."

So what Jesus is actually saying is this:

"Do not worry, saying, 'What shall we eat?' or 'What shall we drink?' or 'What shall we wear?' For the pagans run after all these things, and your heavenly Father knows that you need them. But seek first his kingdom and his righteousness, and all these things will be given to you as well...Therefore, Ask (for the kingdom) and it will be given to you; seek (the kingdom)

*and you will find; knock and the door (to the kingdom) will
be opened to you. For everyone who asks receives; he who seeks
finds; and to him who knocks, the door will be opened". And
when you have found the kingdom and begun living your life
from the consciousness of the kingdom (this is the meaning of
righteousness), all other things (the food, drink, clothes, job,
partner, healing, everything you need to thrive in this world)
will be automatically **added** onto you."*

By becoming aware of your oneness with Infinite Being, you have
entered the kingdom. By consciously knowing that life is the fullness of
God pouring itself into glorious manifestation through you, you have
fulfilled the law of righteousness or faith. Now, all things are yours.

Your intelligent and creative mind is seeking you;
Your ideal healthy body is seeking you;
Your soulmate is seeking you;
Your dream job is seeking you;
Your own thriving business is seeking you;
Your dream home and dream car are seeking you;
The place you want to occupy in history is seeking you;
Those exotic vacations are seeking you;
Great people, friends, and associates are seeking you;
A ceaseless flow of money is seeking you;
The most magnificent version of yourself is seeking you;
Success, wealth, and prosperity, are seeking you.

By observing nature at work, we have arrived at a logical and scientific
· proof of what the Bible reveals as the truth of our being. By knowing the
truth through the evidence of direct experience, we have become free
from the limiting beliefs that used to define and confine our experience
of life. Now that we are free, we can feast in our Father's house as much
as we want, and the supply will never dwindle. It is time to manifest the
miracles we desire.

Now that we have uprooted the old false beliefs, we must now
deliberately replace them with the true ones that we want to manifest in

our lives. For best results, you should spend forty days reprogramming each area of your life. Create a quiet space in which you can have a few minutes of meditation. Meditation here is not used in any religious sense, but rather in reference to the act of quietening your senses, and calming down the activity of your body till you attain a drowsy state. It is in this semi-sleep state that your subconscious mind is most receptive to your suggestions or affirmations, because your conscious mind is quiet.

When you are in the meditative state, repeat to yourself the following affirmations audibly but silently. While doing so, bring yourself into the feeling you would be experiencing if this reality was true for you here and now. The law of salvation says *you must believe in your heart and confess with your mouth*. This simply means that it takes the union of the mental image and the emotion from the heart, to form the spirit of your new reality.

While there is no magic time of day for meditation, the early hours of the morning are usually the best. Two to three times a day is even better, but you should focus on quality, not quantity. It is not a religious exercise, so there is no merit in just following the routine. There is no hard and fast rule about how much time you should spend in meditation or how many times you need to recite your affirmation. The key is to stay in it till your manual activity makes a soul connection. As you say and feel the words, you will get to the point of saturation where it actually feels like "it is done", and you lose the desire to continue in the act. This creative moment or soul connection should be the target of each of your meditation sessions.

The creative moment is the spiritual equivalent of fertilization, and constitutes the point of fusion between the mental image and the emotion, thus the implantation of the new reality in the womb of creation. The reason why you need to repeat the exercise for forty days is because you need to nurture this new seed to grow into a giant tree that will start dropping its fruits into your life automatically. If you sow the seed and go your way, the counter-suggestions of your environment will set in like the rock that will make your seed sprout for a while, then die, or the bird that will eat it up, or the weed that will choke it to death. But if you pray without ceasing for forty days, your seed grows into a giant tree that will prevail as king in the mental forest. When your belief is more powerful than the suggestions from the world around you, you naturally overflow with miracles.

Everything in creation was made for man. Everything in creation is intelligent energy expressed in some specific form, for the fulfillment of a specific purpose, in this gigantic comedy of life. Man is God inhabiting the earth in human form. Thus, man is the operand power of the universe. All things exist to serve man, and all things are restless until they find fulfillment in man's use of them. Of what use would roses be if we had no eyes to appreciate them? Of what use would wine be if we had no tongues to taste it? Of what use would a jet be if there was no one to fly it? Of what use would music be if we had no ears to listen to it?

All things were created before man because they were created for man. And yes, the Genesis version of creation tells us that God planted a garden and placed man in it, and gave him dominion over all that He had created. When you have dominion over something, that thing is constantly preoccupied with pleasing you its master, whether out of love or out of obligation. The metaphor of a new bride and her groom is even better. The universe is a vibrating matrix. The current of this matrix is a vortex pouring toward and through man. Therefore, all things, even the fullness of God, are seeking you.

> *"And to know the love of Christ, which passeth knowledge, that ye might be filled with all the fulness of God." (Ephesians 3:19. KJV).*

When you become aware of the Oneness of Reality, and of yourself as a vortex within this Infinite Ocean of Love, you have found the kingdom of heaven, the Christ in you, which is beyond the surface knowledge of the sense-ruled intellect. When you awaken to the realization that Christ is your Authentic Self, the True Identity of your being, then the fullness of God becomes your living reality, because the Father (Infinity) and the Son (Individuality) are one. This Glorious New You, is the master of the money matrix. This is the hidden treasure you are waking up to.

CHAPTER 12

The Reward

The twelfth insight:

To them that find the hidden treasure, all other things are added. They do not seek success for success is seeking them. They do not ask for wealth for wealth is asking for them. They do not knock on the doors of recognition for recognition is knocking on their doors. They now experience as their reality, a goodness that is exceedingly more than they could have ever asked or imagined.

Later, Ben and Abigail have started a relationship, while Riley is somewhat upset that Ben turned down the 10% finder's fee for the treasure and accepting a much smaller amount that still has netted them all significant wealth.

Riley: *They offered you ten percent, man. Ten percent.*
Ben: *Tell you what- next time we find a treasure that redefines history for all mankind, you call the shots.*
Riley: *What do you care? You got the girl. Enjoy your spoils while I sit on one percent. Half of one percent, actually.[Jumps into red Ferrari]*
Ben:*[Looking at Ferrari]I'm sorry for your suffering, Riley.*

There are people who always have a solution to a problem even before you have finished describing the problem. There are people who always complete their tasks before time and above expectation, even when everyone else is complaining that the time is short, or the task is difficult. We call them geniuses and often wonder how they figure things out so easily, but they will usually tell you that it is just natural. They don't sweat about it.

There are people who come to work before everyone else and leave after everyone else, and always have time to give a helping hand to colleagues who are having a hard time. There are people who spend their time doing the work they love, and money just seems to be irresistibly drawn to them at a constant rate. They don't seem to be working *hard*, but they are always getting richer and richer.

There are people who are never excited to go to the bank on payday, while their colleagues cannot wait for salaries to go through so that they can clear their debts, pay their rents and bills and have some pocket change. They never run short of money.

There are people who are not concerned about having their needs met. They have all that they need to live a comfortable life, and they are always looking out for opportunities to come to the aid of other people in need. They throw parties in their homes regularly, sometimes for 'no good reason'. They grant scholarships to less privileged children, and put money into charity organizations that are dedicated to improving the lives of people by increasing access to health, accommodation, water, electricity, food, etc.

There are people whose names are always among the top ten invited guests at every community event, every fundraising event, every church thanksgiving or project event. And they are always having fun giving. Some of them are usually more excited about giving than others are excited when they receive their paycheck.

There are people who pay cash for their university degree, pay cash for their homes, pay cash for their cars, and are a huge disappointment to the banks because they have the best credibility but are never interested in taking loans. They have income streams that overflow with money even while they sleep.

There are people who are in control of their time. They work when they want and have the freedom to take time off to do the things that are important to them. They spend quality time with their families at home, attend their children's games at school, go to church, volunteer in the community, and go to the gym and beach often.

There are people who take a holiday each year and travel to a different part of the world where they spend weeks living in the best hotels, meeting new people and cultures, visiting amazing touristic, historical and spiritual sites.

There are people who always have a smile on their face because they have peace of mind. They are not afraid of anybody because they don't owe anybody. They are not uncertain about the future because they have enough savings and assets to live comfortably in the old age and still leave more than enough for their children. They are not stressed at work or in business because they are not competing with anybody. They are just 'doing their thing' and having fun with it.

There are people who are as strong and healthy as a bull, as fit as an athlete, as attractive as a super model. They eat and drink what is healthy, yet enjoyable, and have time for exercise and leisure. They wear the clothes and drive the cars that make them glow.

The common denominator about these people is that their life flows effortlessly; they have no money worries; when they want to do something, they focus on the joy it brings to them and others, rather than on the availability of money; they are always inspired, creative, and highly performant in everything they do; and their life just seems magical.

This is not an abstract concept I am presenting here, but the characteristics of a few people that we know. The fact that almost everybody knows at least one such person is proof that such a life is practical and possible. The problem is that the majority of people are not aware that this can, and ought to be their reality. We all admire those who live this way, but most of us have the feeling that it is a special blessing that only a few are endowed with.

The life of freedom, love, joy, peace, and abundance is for all of us, not for a lucky few. Every life form that exists on the earth teaches us the lesson that we are here to thrive. The plants and animals thrive; The sun, moon, and stars thrive; The waters thrive. Only man seems to have a problem with thriving. Success, health and wealth have become a privilege rather than the norm it was designed to be. What could be the problem? How did we find ourselves in a position where the lilies in the fields and the birds in the air are more alive than us humans, the most advanced life form on the planet?

We have built a society that respects and rewards people based on a false sense of value. Now you know that the lines that divide people into classes are arbitrary lines that started as habits within certain communities and developed over time into norms that people now respect without questioning. Come to think of it, if a man is as healthy as a bull, but his head is empty, then he is just that – a bull. So how do you explain why a doctor who repairs the body should have an income that is astronomically higher than that of a teacher who molds the mind?

Take the teacher too and compare him with the bus driver. The teacher teaches a class of fifty students five days a week. The bus driver drives a bus that drops children off to school, and takes them back home, five days a week. Yet when the teacher talks about the driver he refers to him as a 'mere driver', and this attitude reflects on the difference on their paychecks. Perhaps, after the dollar, the second god of the capitalist system is schooling, since pay scales are often graded based on how many years you spent in school to get your qualification.

Such an archaic system is fast losing ground. As the collective consciousness of humans evolves, people are becoming more and more aware of the false laws that have been governing human society and ditching them. It is just a matter of time before enough people rise in consciousness above the illusion. At this stage, the system will crumble by itself. Young people have been so brainwashed that they go through university, graduate and come back home to wait for someone to give them work. That is a great tragedy. Imagine what the world would be if every youth grew up thinking in terms of what he could create to solve a problem in his environment. The human mind is elastic. When you challenge it to create solutions, it obeys you. When you put it to sleep with excuses and complaints, it obeys.

Whether you are a hairdresser, shoemaker, carpenter, teacher, engineer, doctor, lawyer, or church minister; whether you have benefitted from seven or twenty-seven years of formal education; the emerging economy is one that rewards people not according to the titles attached to their names, but according to the value they create in society. Your worth has nothing to do with how much time you have spent in school and by what title you are called. Like Napoleon Bonaparte said, "men are ruled by toys". These decorations are the toys that capitalism has created so that people can be running after them, while turning the machine that is feeding the system.

Refuse to conform to the system that is keeping you down. Forget about the rules you have been following. Burn the script that society has written for you. No matter how old you are, no matter your current status, no matter where you are on this planet, you can follow these steps to write a new story for your life:

- ✓ Realize that the greatest treasure in the universe is the spirit that you are. You are a conscious being that is eternally one with the infinite field of consciousness from which all things flow. There is more gold in your mind than there is in the belly of the earth;
- ✓ Begin to see that the peculiarity of your DNA, the circumstances of your birth and upbringing, your education, your relationships, your adventures, your successes and failures, your gifts and talents, all constitute the complex mix called *you*;
- ✓ Embrace the reality that this *you* is so unique that its exact match has never been, is not, and never will be. Anything that is infused

with this uniqueness automatically becomes special, unique, beyond competition;

✓ Use your uniqueness as your leverage and infuse it into whatever trade you are involved in. This is the power by which you can transmute the ordinary things you do from day to day into a gold mine;

✓ Challenge your brain to give you ideas with which you can turn your trade from a mere job to a venture that serves thousands, possibly millions of people;

✓ Determine to set your own standards in your work and personal life, and live by them, and carry yourself around like royalty.

When you become a genius at an endeavor that makes people's lives easier, healthier, happier, and richer, they will love and respect you. When the number of people thus served get into hundreds, thousands, and millions, that is how you make hundreds, thousands, and millions of dollars and rise in social rank. If you have need for them, you can turn around and hire those who have their degrees as their only security, and they will gratefully bow when you walk in. Let nobody sit anywhere in this world and think that the place where society has placed him is where he is condemned to remain. If you remain there, it is your choice, because I have given you a hint on how to turn yourself from a security guard to a president, or from a good cook at home to the owner of a restaurant chain.

When you awaken to the illusions that have been controlling your life and stand on the mountain top of clarity, every physical thing you are involved in, can serve as a channel for the manifestation of wealth for you. You will join the ranks of those who speak of *income streams* rather than *salaries*. You will be in command of your life, and your money will flow even when you are asleep, because you would have engaged the economic forces to be working for you, rather than you being a slave to the economic forces. And when you are not wasting all your life energies worrying about money, that is when you have the freedom to become truly rich.

Those who have found the hidden treasure are living their ideal life. The ideal life has nothing to do with your level of education, the college you graduated from, your race, your religion, your political party, your gender, or you religion. The ideal life is the life of the truly rich, those who embody the Success Code that we saw at the beginning of this book. When you have found the treasure of life and become truly rich:

1. You are spiritually aware

Ben assumed the identity of a knight. He knew it in his spirit that he was born for something greater than he could imagine. He took upon himself the duty of the Templars and Freemasons and made it his life's purpose to find the National Treasure and complete the mission that had been entrusted on the Gates family.

2. You are mentally sound

Ben studied and equipped his mind adequately for his mission. He did not just float through high school and college like 99% of young people do. He studied with his purpose in mind, and in the course of doing so, gathered the specialized body of knowledge, skills set, and attributes he needed to complete his life's mission.

3. You are emotionally secure

Ben's ability to build and lead a team to help him in his quest, his capacity to detach from the rebellious Ian and move on, the ease with which he charmed Doctor Chase, and the resilience he demonstrated throughout all the trials and setbacks he encountered on his journey, clearly demonstrate a sense of emotional security. Emotionally secure people are at peace with themselves, self-confident, grateful, and joyful. Their inner security is never perturbed by the turbulent circumstances, but rather serve as the compass or guidance star that helps them navigate the storms of life.

4. You are exuding physical health and wellbeing

A healthy spirit expresses itself through a healthy mind. A healthy mind needs a healthy body to serve as the vehicle for its manifestation. Health is not just the absence of disease but a state of physical, mental, emotional, and environmental harmony. Ben clearly demonstrates this quality of sound physical health, fitness, and wellbeing.

5. You are basking in fulfilling relationships

One of the collateral benefits of following his passion and finding the treasure is that Ben ended up in a romantic relationship with Abigail Chase, his relationship with his dad was restored, and he still enjoyed the friendship of Riley.

6. You are in harmony with nature

Harmony with nature is one of the distinguishing qualities of truly rich people. What they eat and drink is as natural as possible. They love to surround themselves with natural environments or take frequent retreats into nature like walking in the woods, swimming, and so on. Ben's taste for a historical house located in the woods with a vast green yard, gives a hint of this attribute.

7. You are thriving in your career

Ben spent the first part of his life seeking the hidden treasure. He did not limit himself to a specific job description in a specific company like most of us do. He was living on purpose. Once he had found the treasure, he became a respected member of the same academic community that used to despise him and his family name. Now he could travel the world giving talks and unveiling the treasure in the museums in which the treasure had been partitioned and displayed. The lesson here is that when you resist the temptation of enslaving yourself with jobs and instead insist on building the career that resonates with your life purpose, you will go through great trials, but if you persist, you will often find yourself at the top in a shorter time.

8. You are financially abundant

Riley is not happy with Ben that he refused to accept the 10% finder's fee for the National Treasure. He settles with something less, but that less is definitely more than he can spend in a lifetime. The size of the National Treasure meant that if Ben had accepted 10% of its value as his reward, then he would have migrated from the problem of "too little money", to the problem of "too much money". He chooses to settle in the middle thereby teaching us a very important lesson; when you have attained true success, you are no longer in the state where you need to covet and hoard money. Money becomes your servant rather than your master.

9. You are spontaneously creative

Creativity really boils down to the ability to spontaneously generate innovative solutions to the problems at hand. Ben demonstrates a heightened sense of creativity throughout the movie, the most sensational creative moment being perhaps his ingenious approach to stealing the Declaration of Independence.

10. You are influential in your community

You are a positive influence in the world. You are a changemaker. By letting the light in you shine, you are inspiring others to allow their light to shine, and together we are transforming the world into the glory of God that it was designed to be. Ben's find is not only a personal victory. He did not just exonerate the name of his family that had been damaged for generations. He became an authority in his field who would be sought after around the world by people who wanted to benefit from his knowledge, skill, and wisdom. He now had enough money and recognition to do any amount of good he wanted to do in the world.

11. You have quality time and freedom to enjoy life

True freedom is when you do not have to work for money and you have no boss to answer to. True freedom is when you have all the money you need to live all the life you are capable of, and the time to put it to good use. Ben is a clear model of this attribute of success.

12. You are perpetually growing and expanding

When you have found the treasure, your experience of life is perpetually increasing, expanding, unfolding, and overflowing. You live in the flow of increasing life, and you are a channel of increase for all. You don't settle and retire because you have attained financial security. Every environment you find yourself in, expands, grows, and gets richer and better. The National Treasure movie depicts this attribute of success by ending with a suspense. Abigail tells Ben she has left a clue in the house for him to decipher. Ben runs after her into the mansion, and the movie ends, leaving us with our imagination to figure out what may happen next.

CHAPTER 13

Summary

In this book we have unveiled a spiritual message that is encoded in the movie "National Treasure". This Gospel of Hollywood as we have called it, is a blueprint for the empowered life. It is hidden in thousands of movies and songs that we watch as mere entertainment, but which are unconsciously programing our minds and souls. Some movies are coded deliberately as a means of getting the message to billions of unsuspecting audiences. In many cases, the creators of the movies stumble on these truths accidentally and express them unknowingly. The key is that when you possess the key with which to decode these truths, entertainment becomes a spiritual retreat, and your life becomes magical. Here are the twelve keys to unlocking the secrets of life as revealed in the movie, "National Treasure":

Step 1: Recognize the fact that there is a higher purpose in life that you are here to serve.

Beyond the material world of eating, drinking, bathing, dressing, walking, talking, and mating, there is a mental world of waking, sleeping, dreaming. Beyond the mental world of waking, sleeping, and dreaming, there is a spiritual world that constitutes the womb of creation, the boundless field in which unspoken treasures are buried. Those who become masters, heroes, inventors, and truly successful people are those who tear through the veils of the physical and mental and dive into the living waters of the spirit.

Step 2: Become aware that there is a power within you that is greater than the circumstances in which you find yourself.

Within each one of us lies a knight, a genius, a giant, an avatar, a messiah, waiting to be born. What we are born into is a socially constructed hallucination in which we are programmed to sleep-walk through life, not knowing who we truly are and what we came here to do. The moment we wake up from the dream of materiality and recognize that we have been living a lie, the miracle begins to happen. The Christ within us begins to unfold and life starts becoming magical. The secret of life is to awaken this knight within you. The magic of life is to become the Christ that is your real self. This is the treasure that once found, gives you everything else worth finding in life.

Step 3: Outgrow your limited concept of good and evil, give up your fear, and begin to see the contrasts in life is the field in which desire is born and experience is created.

Good and evil are not opposites. They are the two sides of the coin of life. Just as we cannot appreciate the light without the background darkness, evil is the contrast against which the good erupts and is experienced. Whatsoever is negative in our life is there to point us to its contrast that we are desiring to experience. Rather than fight the negative, our job is to intend its opposite and pursue it. Become aware of what you do not want. Then, instead of fighting it or trying to solve it, use it as the contrast to define and clarify what you do want. Then shift your awareness to that which you do want, and immerse yourself into becoming it.

Step 4: Understand that inertia is the natural state of life, and that in order for you to get anything done, you must first conquer the mental conditioning that your environment has imprisoned you in.

We are all products of conditioning. Our genetics and environment have programmed into our subconscious minds the belief system or paradigm from which we think, feel, speak, act, and interact with the world. The paradigm is the lens through which we perceive the world, and the conditioner of our automatic responses. For the most part we are sleep-walking through life because more than 95% of our activities are spontaneous expressions of our subconscious programming. Our conditioned reality is the comfort zone in which we live most of our lives. Because we are not aware of what is going on, we have no desire for change, and most times we even resist change.

Step 5: Rely on your imagination, not on the evidence of the senses.

In the preservation room of social conditioning, our thinking capacities are embalmed so that instead of using our brains to think, we use them to conform. Studying means wiring our brains after the pattern that has been laid down by the curriculum. Being religious means wiring our brains after the pattern that has been laid down by the creed, dogmas, and scriptures. Being a political activist means wiring our brains after the pattern that has been laid down by the agenda of the party. Modern man does not think, yet thinking is the one capacity that makes men gods. The mental programs that have been conditioned into us precipitate as our bodies and the unconscious habits of our bodies account for almost 95% of our daily lives. The path of success lies in the direction of waking up from this sense-consciousness and training yourself to work with your imagination or intuition which is the sense of the spirit.

Step 6: Pursue your purpose with unapologetic passion and uncompromising persistence.

In order for the things in your life to change, you must change the things in your life. You must become "white hot" with desire in order to trigger the laws by which your mind begins orchestrating the universe to bring about the good you desire. We spend our lives complaining about our circumstances and hoping that our lives will change the day the things outside of us change – the government, our employer, our partner, the economy, and so on. What we fail to realize is that nothing changes for us unless we change who we are. The universe is always matching our experience with the state we are occupying in consciousness. In order for us to see a change, we must be the change. And the key is in the 3Ps: Passion, Purpose, Persistence.

Step 7: Leverage the power of synchronicity by immersing your head, heart, and hand in the thing you do.

When you pursue your purpose with passion, you eventually get to the place where you are so immersed in your quest that it is as if it is the purpose that now possesses you. At this stage you lose touch with time, fear, doubt, and worry, and your life flows like a river. This is the state called synchronicity. You are in a state of resonance with the universe, such that the universe is now orchestrating itself to work in your favor. Synchronicity is another name for miracles. It is not something that comes to you by chance or luck or as a favor from some far-off God. You can deliberately organize your life in such a way that the law of synchronicity or resonance pour miracles into your laps as a daily occurrence.

Step 8: Change your concept of failure. See adversity is the universe dismantling the things that exist in order to repackage that which is coming to you.

The reason why we think in terms of success and failure is because we subconsciously assume that life is a straight line. When we do not get what we want, when we want it, how we want it, and where we want it, we say that we have failed. Other times we call ourselves failures because we are comparing ourselves with other people and using their story as the standard for our own life. The truth is that there is no such thing as failure. What appears as failure are only setbacks and detours that the universe places on our path to redirect us to where we should be going. Your gift lies within your story. Your opportunity lies within your adversity. If you embrace your challenges and really contemplate them rather than run away from them, you will find the secret key hidden within them for you.

Step 9: Expand your consciousness to match the good you are desiring.

Ignorance resulting from conditioned consciousness is the root of all fear, stress, hate, disease, poverty, and failure. There is a realm of expanded consciousness beyond the doctrines of our social institutions and physical life. You enter the realm of expanded consciousness by realizing that the conditioned consciousness is false. It is only from the realm of expanded consciousness that you can transform your life. Albert Einstein once said that the significant problems we face cannot be solved at the same level of consciousness that we were in when we created the problem. Everything boils down to a shift in awareness. Life is not really about you achieving new things, but rather about you having new experiences as a result of becoming a new you.

Step 10: When the night gets darkest, do not give up. That is when the dawn begins to break.

Just as dawn is preceded by midnight, just as the germination of a new plant is preceded by the death of the seed, just as the birth of the butterfly is preceded by the death of the caterpillar, the finding of the treasure of life is preceded by a dead end, a Calvary experience, or what is often termed the dark night of the soul. It is out of this darkness that the new self emerges.

In the very moment when you feel like fainting, in the very instant where you feel like your night is at its darkest, in that very experience when you feel like you are in the belly of hell itself, it is there that you will find the treasure you have been seeking. Your life story, no matter how tragic, is the container of your gift. Look for it and you will find it.

Step 11: Be open to receive your good. Live in a state of expectancy, gratitude, and love.

When you ask, it is automatically and unconditionally given. Through the Law of Correspondence, the universe is forever mirroring the state of being that you have created in your awareness. Through the Law of

Attraction, the universe orchestrates itself to deliver into your experience the people, places, events, circumstances, and experiences that vibrate at the same frequency as the reality you have created for yourself. The only thing left is for you to receive. In order to receive you must be in the state of "allowing" or what is also termed "flow". Love is the most sublime state that the soul can experience. Love blossoms in the body as joy, and joy exudes the fragrance of gratitude or service. To be in the ideal state in which your good will come to you effortlessly, therefore, fill your being with love, joy, and gratitude.

Step 12: Enjoy every moment that life gives to you, and as you do so, you will find yourself expanding into ever increasing goodness.

To them that find the hidden treasure, all other things are added. They do not seek success for success is seeking them. They do not ask for wealth for wealth is asking for them. They do not knock on the doors of recognition for recognition is knocking on their doors. They now experience as their reality, a goodness that is exceedingly more than they could have ever asked or imagined.

Success is not some colossal achievement that will come your way in some distant future. While you may have many such experiences along the way, they are just sign posts on the journey of life. real success is a state you live in, a journey you are undertaking. The Success Code that we examined at the beginning of this book is a blueprint that you can use to recreate your life in such a way that no matter who you are, where you are, what you have, or what you don't have, you can begin right now, to experience the joy of one who has found the hidden treasure.

THE END

Printed in the United States
By Bookmasters